SEEDS *of* PROMISE

The Prophetic Church
in Central America

GUILLERMO MELÉNDEZ

Friendship Press • **New York**

© 1990 by Friendship Press
Editorial Offices:
475 Riverside Drive, Room 772, New York, NY 10115
Distribution Offices:
P.O. Box 37844, Cincinnati, OH 45222-0844

Manufactured in the United States of America
94 93 92 91 90   5 4 3 2 1

Library of Congress Cataloging in Publication Data

Meléndez, Guillermo.
    Seeds of promise: the prophetic church in Central America/
Guillermo Meléndez.
        p. cm.
    Includes bibliographical references.
    ISBN 0-377-00204-6
    1. Catholic Church—Central America—History—20th century. 2. Central
America—Church history—20th century. 3. Revolutions—Religious aspects—
Catholic Church. 4. Liberation theology. 5. Catholic Church—Doctrines.
I. Title.
BX1432 .M46   1990
282'.728' 09045—dc20
                                                            89-48934

Contents

Publisher's Acknowledgments

Friendship Press is grateful to Guillermo Meléndez for his willingness to take on this project, for his gifts as a historian and theologian, and, above all, for his commitment to the people of Central America and the faith that is being renewed through their struggles. We appreciate the assistance he received in his research and analysis from colleagues in Central America and elsewhere, both through their writings and in person.

We are also grateful for the author's graciousness in granting translators and editors the scope they might need to prepare *Seeds of Promise* for North American readers. In doing this, we have sought to remain faithful to the integrity of the author's presentation, based on his thoughtful observations as a Christian in Central America. We have worked to maintain this integrity while assuring that the complex reality faced by Central American Christians is as available as possible to readers who have not yet encountered that reality in person — and also to some who have and who can compare their experience with models presented here.

Several people have brought special gifts to this preparation. Elice Higgenbotham did the initial translation and read the manuscript at several stages with helpful comments. Moira Ojeda assisted with some of the translation. Mission educators of several U.S. and Canadian denominations reviewed the manuscript. Editor John Eagleson brought his extensive knowledge of Latin American theology, his facility in both Spanish and English, and his technical magic in computer typesetting. Editor Carol Ames practiced creative sentence revision and shared her questions as a nonexpert on Central America. Don Burgard, who wrote the "boxes" of background in Chapter 2, drew together salient information about five nations and condensed it into very limited space.

All of us appreciate how much we have learned as this book was prepared for publication. Most of all, we have been nourished and challenged by a new encounter with prophetic witness of courageous Christians.

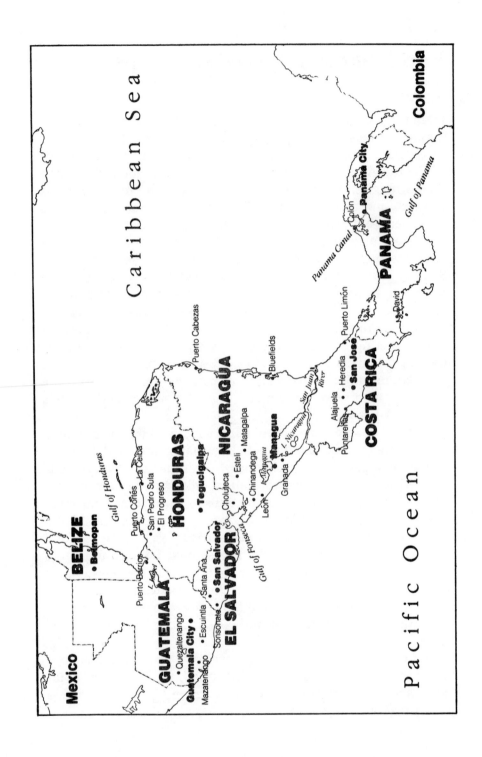

Chapter 1

Understanding the Church

The birth of the prophetic church has played a crucial role in the transformation of Central American society. This coming-into-existence was not like planting a cross to claim a certain area of land or like setting a cornerstone for a particular building, because the prophetic church has grown up among already established Christian groups. Rather, it has been more like seeds carried by the wind of the Spirit — to the people of tiny rural villages, to refugee camps, even to cathedrals.

Here we will look with some detail at the ground where this church has taken root, at those who have prepared the soil and watered the seed, and — as in Jesus' parable — at the rocky pathways, the thorns and thistles that choke the growth of the prophetic church. To do so, we will describe with care the Central American social and political setting as well as the various theologies that will help us understand the role of Christians.

Several difficulties are involved in trying to sketch in a small book the broad strokes of the birth and recent history of the prophetic church in Central America.

The first is due to *the differences among the countries*, each with its own social, political, and cultural characteristics. Although probably in no other region of Latin America are there so many points of unity, there are profound differences between countries on the Central American isthmus and within the countries themselves, differences that cannot be forgotten when we make general statements.

A second difficulty involves *the diversity of positions within the churches*, within the countries and in the region as a whole. Because of this diversity, any general affirmation about *the* Central American church can be misleading.

Another difficulty involves the need *to identify at least in some way what we understand by the term "church,"* in both its the-

1

ological and sociological meanings. We must distinguish the different spheres within the institutional church — the hierarchy (that is, the leadership), the intermediate level, and the grass-roots — while keeping in mind their mutual relationships and interdependence. We must differentiate between discourse and practice, that is, between what the churches say and what they do. We must be careful not to interpret a church simply on the basis of what it says in its documents without also considering its social practice, both in society and within the church itself. We must be careful not to affirm of the whole church something true only of its hierarchy — or of a part of it — or, on the other hand, to attribute to the whole church something true of just a part of the church on the grassroots level.

The fourth difficulty to bear in mind is *the great diversity of Christian churches* present in the area. Although Roman Catholicism still is the majority and predominant church, we need to be aware of the presence and important role played by other Christian churches that are linked to organizations like the World Council of Churches (WCC) and the Latin American Council of Churches (Consejo Latinoamericano de Iglesias, CLAI), or the more conservative Latin American Evangelical Fellowship (Confraternidad Evangélica Latinoamericana, CONELA). There are also numerous Protestant sects in Central America, principally of U.S. origin. Many are supported with significant human and economic resources by those who consider the sects useful in counteracting the influence of prophetic Christianity, both Roman Catholic and Protestant. However, because Protestants have traditionally been a religious minority in Central America, and though growing in numbers still remain so (from 3 to 20 percent, depending on the area), our references to "the church" refer principally to the Roman Catholic Church.[1]

Another difficulty is related to the important *non-Christian religious expressions* in the region. Some of these originated in pre-Columbian societies, that is, societies predating the arrival of the Europeans; these expressions are encountered above all

---

[1]See Carmelo Alvárez and Carlos Tamez, *People of Hope: The Protestant Movement in Central America* (New York: Friendship Press, 1990).

among the indigenous and peasant[2] population. Other non-Christian beliefs and practices originated among black peoples who immigrated or were forcibly brought to the area, principally on the Caribbean coast. These expressions often exist along with Christian influences in various combinations.

Our Method of Analysis

The prophetic church (often called "the popular church," that is, the church that is of the people) in Central America has had an influence that goes far beyond the relatively small number of people involved directly in it. And it is intimately connected to the realities of life and to the institutional church in Central America. To look at the prophetic church we need a method, a framework, that helps us see the patterns within a complex situation and to see them as accurately as possible.[3]

In doing this we want to avoid two very frequent errors. On the one hand, it is a mistake to try to interpret the church by considering it simply in itself, with no relationship to other economic, political, social, or cultural factors. On the other hand, it is an error to consider the church *only* in political terms.

So our method has two principles. First we assert that the institutional church — at all levels — is part of society; that is, it participates in all the economic, political, social, and cultural processes of the society in which it is immersed. Second, we assert that the church is also relatively autonomous (that is, it engages in activities peculiarly its own, even its own specific internal conflicts). Thus it can participate in society as the church, with its own specific identity.

The relationship between the church and society is dynamic and interactive. So we need to keep three perspectives in mind: the church as a product of society; the church in its relative autonomy; and the church as an actor in society, either reinforcing the current social order or working to transform it.

---

[2]The English term "peasant" is used throughout to translate the Spanish word *campesino*, which means one who lives in the *campo*, or countryside.

[3]For a more thorough presentation of this methodology, see Pablo Richard, *Death of Christendoms, Birth of the Church: Historical Analysis and Theological Interpretation of the Church in Latin America* (Maryknoll, N.Y.: Orbis Books, 1987).

We will be giving special consideration to two fundamental relationships: (1) the relationship between the church and the hierarchy-government-ruling class, and (2) the relationship between the church and the people's movement.[4]

In looking at the first relationship, we'll consider how the church hierarchy has provided credibility to governments, and the nature of the alliance it has established with the ruling classes. In Central America the alliance between the Roman Catholic Church and the state is a well-established tradition. Here we want to highlight where there has been a breakdown in that traditional relationship between the hierarchical church, on the one hand, and the governments and the ruling classes on the other.

Second, we will try to interpret the relationship between the prophetic church and the people's movement. How have Christians and Christian communities participated in the people's movement and how has the people's movement had an impact on Christians and their communities? How has the preaching of a gospel of liberation influenced society as a whole, and how has increased political awareness among the poor and exploited people had an impact on religious awareness?

These two relationships are not parallel, but they do have important effects on each other. Any change in the relationship between the church and the state directly influences the grassroots church. In the same way, the development of a grassroots church movement puts pressure on the existing relationship between the church hierarchy and the ruling classes.

Models of the Church

When we speak of the "church" in this book, we are referring directly to church structures, at both hierarchical and grassroots levels. In the Roman Catholic Church, among the hierarchical structures we include, at the local level, the bishops, priests, and the brothers and sisters in religious orders, as well as other

---

[4]The "people's movement" (*movimiento popular*) refers to groups and networks organized at the grassroots level, especially among the poor, to struggle for economic justice and political participation. It is also frequently referred to in this book as the "grassroots movement."

ministries and responsibilities exercised by laypeople; at the national level, the bishops' conferences and religious orders; at the regional level, the Central American Bishops' Secretariat (SEDAC); and, at the Latin American level, the Latin American Bishops Council (CELAM) and similar continent-wide organizations. Among the grassroots church structures we consider principally parishes, the Christian base communities,[5] and local church organizations, as well as other movements and organizations directly linked with the hierarchy.

All Protestant churches have structures, although these vary widely and are not easily categorized. Some have bishops, some are connected through governing groups that perform the functions of bishops, some associate with one another less structurally, and some claim congregational autonomy. Even among those denominations with less formal structures, some place considerable authority in the clergy. Many have relationships to regional and international denominational and ecumenical organizations. In some cases, especially among Protestant groups or sects that have established a presence in Central America more recently, the "structures" include extensive reliance on funding and direction from countries outside the region, especially from "parent" churches in the U.S. Moreover, even well-established Protestant churches in Central America have fewer centuries of regional tradition and traditional structuring than does the Roman Catholic Church. And because all have fewer members, there is less "distance" between leadership and the grassroots level. Churches of all denominations have formal or informal centers of power, although the analysis of "church" here applies more directly to the history and organization of the Roman Catholic Church.

In recent years theologians — especially theologians of liberation — and Latin American church historians have been working out various models to better understand the church and its relationship to society, that is, to better understand its different ways of being the church, both in its internal structures and in its relationship with society.[6]

---

[5]See below, p. 8

[6]Peruvian theologian Gustavo Gutiérrez, for example, presents four models

We also need to make it clear that these models do not designate actual churches. They are different ways of conceiving of the church or of living as the church. Normally, they coexist in a contradictory way in any given specific church. The reality of the churches is much more complex and dynamic than our terminology. Our models are simply instruments for analysis; they do not refer to some static and unchanging structure.

To interpret the Central American church, theologian Pablo Richard proposes two models: the church of Christendom and the prophetic church, or the church of the poor.

The Church of Christendom

In the Christendom model, the fundamental relationship is the church-power relationship; this relationship orients both the presence of the church in society and the internal structuring of the church itself. In the church of Christendom, ecclesiastical authority seeks to have the church influence society through the political and social power of the ruling classes. Internally, this church organizes itself in clearly defined levels of authority and power.

The church of Christendom tries to utilize all the economic, social, political, legal, cultural, and religious structures of the dominant system, because it believes it thus can increase its "Christianizing" presence in society. It possesses a true mission, but that mission is corrupted because it depends on the use of power. The church of Christendom seeks to "Christianize" the ruling elites through education and the family. It hopes to form a "Christian" ruling class (or a "Catholic" one in the case of the Roman Catholic Church), from which future leaders, generals, judges, and business persons will come, assuring the presence and power of the church in society. In this model of church, regardless of the good intentions of its defenders, the bishops and clergy must always seek close relations with governments and ruling classes. For the church of Christendom, therefore, any

for ways the church has responded to the world (see *A Theology of Liberation: History, Politics, and Salvation*, rev. ed. (Maryknoll, N.Y.: Orbis Books, 1988), pp. 34–46. Leonardo Boff also analyzes four models of the Reign-World-Church model in *Church, Charism, Power: Liberation Theology and the Institutional Church* (New York: Crossroad, 1985).

break with political power and the ruling classes is practically unthinkable, because that would mean a loss of possibilities for its mission.

In the Christendom model, relationships within the church tend to be authoritarian, bureaucratic, and clerical. The church structure is involved principally with worship and pastoral care, because the prophetic element is diminished almost to the point of disappearing.

The Prophetic Church

In the prophetic church model, on the other hand, the church relates to the whole of society through its presence among oppressed groups and the exploited classes. The church itself is organized according to relationships of fellowship and service. In this model it is essential that the church not use political power in its mission or in its internal organization, but rather rely on the power of its faith, its hope, and its charity, that is, the power of the gospel. In this model the church of course also must have ways to organize and fund itself, but its mission does not depend on these means. This way of being church is not so much a well-defined model as it is a church renewal movement, the church again finding its true self. In the prophetic church model, the relationship between the church and life itself, above all the life of the impoverished and threatened majority, is the essential relationship.

We need to emphasize that the prophetic church is not, as the media often affirm, a parallel, rebel, or clandestine church. It is neither an alternative nor an anti-institutional or anti-hierarchical church. The prophetic church is simply another model of church, that is, another way of living, organizing, and thinking about the actual, existing church.

Also, the prophetic church is universal and not sectarian. It calls upon all people, but in different ways. It strives to save the poor by freeing them from their poverty, while it strives to save the rich by freeing them of their wealth and of all their means of exploitation and domination.

We have chosen to call this church born from the people "prophetic" because this model recovers the biblical tradition of the prophets' cry for justice for the downtrodden and their trust in God's requirement that the covenant community care especially for the poor. This is the tradition that Jesus and the gospel writers also claimed for themselves. This model of the church is prophetic also because it looks to God's promise of "a future and a hope" (Jeremiah 29:11) and the people's call to participate in establishing God's Reign of justice, mercy, and peace.[7]

The central objective of this book is to show how this prophetic church has arisen and evolved over the last thirty years in Central America.

Looking at the development of the prophetic church will mean that we will pay attention at the same time to another objective of this book: to interpret the response of the traditional church to the Central American situation. We will see how the Christendom model of the church is being rebuilt in Central America. This is why we take time to examine the relationship between the church hierarchy and the ruling social and political power. As we pursue these objectives, we need to be aware that both "models" of the church include people and groups with a great variety of attitudes and approaches to their faith and their societies. Neither model comprises a completely homogeneous set of people or organizations. Also, neither model is set in concrete — both are still growing and changing.

Christian Base Communities

Finally, when we explore the prophetic church model, we will need to have some understanding of the Christian base communities, which have been crucial to the development of this model. One very real difficulty for understanding the meaning of the expression "Christian base community" is that the term is applied to very different realities. And it is practically impossible to give a definition that covers the entire multifaceted phenomenon of the Christian base communities.[8] Attempts at definition are trying to describe a reality that is dynamic, dif-

---

[7] For further reflection on the nature of the prophetic church model, see chapter 5, especially pp. 60–62, and chapter 9, especially pp. 120–123

[8] "Christian base communities" is the English term used here to translate the Spanish *comunidades eclesiales de base*.

ferent, and new, more than to enclose its rich content in a rigid formula.

We can say that a Christian base community is a *community*, with a clear *Christian* and *ecclesial* consciousness, built on a *base* (for example, a neighborhood, a village, an estate).[9] The Christian base communities are communities because they bring together persons who have the same faith and live in the same geographical area or work at the same site. Motivated by their faith, they carry out a life in community with its problems, struggles, longings, and hopes for liberation. The communities are Christian and ecclesial because they gather as the church, as basic units of the community of faith, hope, and charity. They are of the base because they are comprised of people who belong to the "lowest" layers of society. To sum up, when Latin American Christians organize themselves as Christian base communities, they do so in order to live, confess, communicate, reflect on, and celebrate their faith communally. The Christian base communities arise among the poor people or within the people's movement, that is, "the people on the move."

The Christian base communities are a channel for what has been called the "in-breaking" of the poor in the church. When this occurs, the poor are present in the church, not simply as "religious clientele" or a mute mass, but rather as active agents who imprint a people's identity upon the church in its language and symbols, in its priorities and practices. The emergence of this new identity is highly complex and uneven, because the people themselves represent diverse social and cultural groups.

The new prophetic church model encourages, guides, and strengthens this kind of Christian living in the Christian base communities. The prophetic church is built on these communities, but, as Pablo Richard points out, it is not identical to these communities. It includes them, but it is much more: the prophetic church embraces all the liberating and transforming impact of the Christian base communities among poor Christians and throughout the rest of society as well.

---

[9] See Frei Betto, *O que é comunidade eclesial de base?* (São Paulo: Ed. Brasiliense, 1981).

Chapter 2

The Land and the People

If we include in the term "Central America" those countries with a shared past, a history lived in common, then we refer to five countries: Guatemala, El Salvador, Honduras, Nicaragua, and Costa Rica. Panama and Belize now are part of Central America, but their belonging to the region is very recent. So we shall refer to Panama or Belize only when their situation is significant for Central America as a whole.

The territory consists of 419,000 square kilometers (a little larger than California but less than half the size of Ontario), representing scarcely 2 percent of the Latin American land mass. Its approximately 23 million inhabitants (less than the population of California or of Canada) make up 6 percent of the total population of Latin America. Although some economic advances have given Costa Rica a per capita income somewhat higher than that of the rest of Latin America, the Central American countries as a whole are among the poorest and most underdeveloped of Latin America.

A Geography of Contrasts

Central America presents great geographical contrasts. The most accentuated difference throughout the isthmus is between the central mountainous regions, whose slopes descend smoothly to the Pacific coast, and the plains of the Caribbean coast, with their hot, rainy climate and abundant vegetation. Types of soil also vary greatly. In the central region and along the Pacific coast the soil is of volcanic origin. These regions enjoy a relatively temperate climate with well-distributed precipitation between the dry and rainy seasons. In the Caribbean region there are permanent drainage problems and natural threats from decay and disease. So the central highlands and the Pacific coastal mountainsides are a more favorable natural setting for agriculture and for sustaining populations of some density.

With the possible exception of the San Juan River, on the border between Costa Rica and Nicaragua, there are practically no large navigable rivers and few natural deep-water ports. The mountains have always made overland communication difficult. On the other hand, water travel has never represented a very efficient alternative for the people concentrated in the central highlands, relatively distant from the coasts, or for those of the Pacific coast, with few good ports.

Learning to survive with natural disasters is also an unavoidable part of Central American life. Earthquakes and volcanic eruptions on the Pacific side and in the central highlands have presented an endless succession of destruction and catastrophes. On the Caribbean side the people face devastation by hurricanes and tropical storms.

Central America has great political and strategic importance. Panama, in particular, at the narrowest part of the isthmus, has been an important transit point since colonial times, when the Spanish began to derive fabulous wealth from the mines of the viceroyalty of Peru; the gold arrived on the West coast of Central America by sea. Overland transport across the isthmus required an enormous mobilization of mules as well as a vast apparatus of defense against constant attacks by English, French, and Dutch pirates. The Central American countries supplied the necessary mules and provisions, but the decline of Peruvian mining after 1650 drastically reduced the need for such supplies and reinforced the isolation of the area.

Beginning in the early seventeenth century, pirates marauded in the Bay of Honduras — on the Caribbean coast — and had their hideouts in the Mosquitia[1] and Belize. This area's large forests of precious woods brought English traders, who established permanent settlements. These in turn became bases for contraband and, in the case of the Mosquitia, for harassment of Spanish galleons and of nearby Spanish colonies.

The various English and other settlements on the Caribbean coast were augmented by Afro-Caribbean peoples, mostly from

---

[1]The Mosquitia is an area on the Caribbean coast extending from Cape Honduras to the Matina River in Costa Rica. Its name comes from the Mosquito, or Miskito, people, who were the original inhabitants of the region.

GUATEMALA

Four thousand years ago, the area that is now Guatemala, southern Mexico, Belize, El Salvador, and Honduras was home to many tribes collectively known as the Maya. Between 250 and 900 C.E., Mayan civilization flourished. The Maya developed an elaborate religious worldview, influenced by their advances in astronomy, mathematics, chronology, and hieroglyphic writing. They constructed a solar calendar remarkable for its accuracy as well as tables plotting solar eclipses and the movements of Venus and the moon.

Around 900 C.E., for reasons still unknown, Mayan civilization began to decline. When the Spanish arrived in the early 1500s, they were able to exploit the Maya's vulnerability, capturing many for slavery and ruling the rest. Large numbers died from the conquerors' European diseases, to which they had no immunity. The Spanish also forced the people to produce goods for sale in Spain and in other colonies. Most of the area's resources were soon in the hands of the Spanish.

In Guatemala alone did the indigenous people survive this conquest in large numbers. When Spanish became the predominant language of these new colonies, people in rural Guatemala plus a few other remote areas retained their native languages and religion. However, the Spanish confiscated the lowlands for their own use, forcing the indigenous people to retreat to the highlands, where they lived in defensive isolation. Today the indigenous people comprise over half the population, but are the victims of racial discrimination.

When Mexico became independent from Spain in 1821, Central America followed suit and subsequently joined the Mexican Empire. But in less than two years, Central America declared its independence from Mexico. A union called the United Provinces of Central America also proved temporary, and in 1838 the organization split into Guatemala, Honduras, El Salvador, Nicaragua, and Costa Rica.

In the years following independence, dictator and president Justo Rufino Barrios (1873–85) effected a modernization plan for Guatemala, building roads and railways and establishing both a national army and an adequate banking system. But the Roman Catholic church suffered a blow from which it has never fully recovered. Barrios exiled the Jesuits and much of the church leadership and confiscated much church property and land, which, along with confiscated Indian land, he later offered to wealthy landowners for coffee plantations. Coffee exports are now responsible for nearly half the nation's revenues.

A series of dictatorships ended in 1944, when a group of students and young professionals forced President Jorge Ubico to resign. After Ubico's immediate successor was ousted later in 1944, Juan José Arévalo became Guatemala's first democratically elected president. Although he initiated reforms in education and health and attempted to transfer power from the military to organized labor and other popular groups, he failed to address the fundamental injustice of Guatemalan society — the unequal distribution of land.

In 1952, the next president, Jacobo Arbenz (1951–54), undertook a bold reform program that included formation of over eight hundred peasant organizations and land redistribution. Arbenz also confiscated property belonging to the United Fruit Company. He offered to compensate the U.S.-owned company at its own declared taxable value. But several members of the Eisenhower administration had strong ties to United Fruit. This, coupled with Guatemalan communists' role in Arbenz's government, brought U.S. reaction. In 1953 the CIA began a campaign of disinformation and destabilization in Guatemala, and in 1954 it sponsored an invasion by Guatemalan exiles that ended with Arbenz's resignation.

From 1954 to 1986, Guatemala was governed by a succession of military leaders. Julio César Méndez Montenegro (1966–70) was the sole civilian exception, but even he could not govern without the military. Under these military governments Guatemalan peasants, most of them Indians, suffered dislocation, bombings of their villages, kidnappings, torture, and murder. At Panzos in 1978 several hundred Indians had gathered to hear the government's response to their letter protesting their impending eviction from their land. The government's response was gunfire. Over one hundred Indians were killed — and buried in mass graves that the army had dug beforehand.

Despite the election of a civilian president in 1985, the military remains strong, considering itself the protector of Guatemala's new civilian democracy. However, if this new democracy fails to satisfy demands for peace and prosperity, the military is fully prepared to assume the control they have given up. The presidency of Vinicio Cerezo has disappointed many Guatemalans, and the problems of poor health care, poverty, and the gap between rich and poor have only increased during this time. After a brief decline, the number of reported human rights violations has increased: in 1988 Guatemala topped the Council on Hemispheric Affairs' list of Latin American countries with human rights violations. As old issues are raised once again, Guatemala will surely be visible as a nation of suffering and hope.

Jamaica (an English possession from 1655). At the end of the nineteenth century, expanding banana plantations and railroad construction — in the hands of U.S. enterprises — caused a new Afro-Caribbean migration, especially from Jamaica, along with the arrival of some contingents of Chinese workers. This population of the Caribbean region added new cultures and profound contrast to Central America.

Toward the middle of the nineteenth century, rivalry for development and control of a trade route linking the Atlantic and the Pacific again brought to the fore the strategic importance of the isthmus. There were two principal options: a connection via the south of Nicaragua, taking advantage of the navigable San Juan River and Lake Cocibolca, and the old colonial route through what is now Panama. The balance of power began to tilt toward the U.S., and after its triumph in its war against Spain (1898), it became the controlling presence in the Caribbean. The contrived "independence" of Panama as a nation separate from Colombia (1903) and the immediate negotiation of a canal treaty (the Canal was opened in 1914) completed the basic elements of U.S. control.

The defense and security of the Panama Canal then became the key objective of U.S. foreign policy in the region. The steps toward liberation taken by Augusto César Sandino in Nicaragua in the late 1920s, the Salvadoran peasant revolt (1932), the great banana strikes of 1934 in Costa Rica and Honduras, and similar events caused Central America to be perceived as a turbulent and unstable region where "pacification" had to be imposed at any cost. The Cuban revolution of 1959 and the Central American liberation movements have become important factors in this overall picture. In recent years the whole Caribbean–Central American area has experienced an intense process of economic crisis, social protest, and nationalist struggles that have presented a serious and growing challenge to U.S. control in the region.

A Rural and Remote World

The base of the Central American economy has always been subsistence agriculture. The majority of the population has worked to grow the crops they and their families need to survive. Onto this economic base, larger landowners imposed the cultivation of various export crops, all of which soon exhausted the resources of the soil. In the second half of the nineteenth century, coffee and bananas became the principal export crops.

A continuous theme common to the area's history is pillage of natural resources. After the near annihilation of the aboriginal population in the sixteenth century, the inexorable sacking of forests began, and it continues to this day. Recently, animals on the land and the sea have also been affected; vast areas are — or soon will be — ecological wastelands.

Central America never had a monopoly on valuable products. Furthermore, the costs of production and transportation of its exportable goods put it at a disadvantage in comparison with other regions of Latin America. Its integration into the colonial commercial circuits was limited, and very early it was considered a territory of marginal value.

The cycles of exported goods — brief because each succeeding commodity exhausted the land — contributed to the perennial weakness of government power, another structural thread in Central American history. This helps explain the extremely violent means used to gain power and social control, almost exclusively for the benefit of the ruling classes. The land grantees of the early colonial era, the indigo merchants of the eighteenth century, and the modern exporters of coffee and bananas share this enormous accumulation of private privileges.

Culture and Religion. Both the pre-Columbian cultures and the Afro-Caribbean population are subjugated, alienated cultures, cut off from their roots. Achievement of a cultural identity has been impossible for these groups, because racial-ethnic prejudice has so often been used to justify the inferior status of the great majority. Exclusion of the indigenous and black people — and, to a lesser degree, the Chinese — became an invariable social rule, relying on various subtle or open methods of segregation. This discrimination lasted well into this century (and some persists to this day).

An element central to colonial and neocolonial domination was the churches' power to shape people's thinking. In its teaching and practice the Roman Catholic Church supported a society controlled by a powerful privileged class. National governments

H O N D U R A S

Prior to the arrival of the Spanish, Honduras was home to several Maya tribes. One tribe established the flourishing city of Copán, near the present-day Guatemalan border. Today Copán is revealing a wealth of new archaeological information on the Maya. Unlike Guatemala, Honduras has few surviving indigenous peoples. Most of the population is of mixed Indian and Spanish descent (*mestizo*).

After the United Provinces of Central American dissolved in 1838, Honduras experienced disunity and instability as conservative and liberal factions fought for control of the country and its Central American neighbors frequently interfered in its internal affairs. In 1876 two Honduran members of the Guatemalan cabinet returned to their country and initiated a program to draw Honduras into the world economy. The plan was based on granting economic concessions to foreign investors in mining. It was hoped that partnerships between foreigners and local investors would develop mining technology and make mining a profitable industry. However, the combination of concessions and lack of Honduran capital allowed foreign companies to take over the industry completely.

The economic void created when the mining industry collapsed just before the turn of the century was filled by the banana industry. Because the Honduran economy remained so short of capital, independent local banana producers were quickly driven out of business by large companies. By 1929 two of these companies, United Fruit and Standard Fruit, with their subsidiaries owned or controlled 650,000 acres in Honduras (about 2.5 percent of the country). Because this land had previously been uninhabited jungle, peasants were not dispossessed of their land.

The banana companies entered Honduras with relative ease and quickly dominated more than just the country's export economy. Indeed, the history of Honduran government from the late nineteenth century on is inextricably linked to these and other multinational corporations. From their beginnings they have exercised enormous control over the government. For example, the government granted the companies large extensions of land because they promised to build railroads. Consistently claiming losses, the companies laid only fifty miles of railway in thirty years. At the same time, they were enjoying large tax breaks and even government subsidies. In the 1890s the salary of President Marco Aurelio Soto was paid by the Rosario Mining Company. While such blatant evidence of corporate control is less evident today, as recently as 1975 United Brands (formerly United Fruit) paid the government a bribe of $1.25 million to avoid a tax of $1.50 per box of bananas.

In contrast to its neighbors, for most of its history the Honduran military has remained relatively weak. The country's economy did not create the conditions conducive to a strong centralized military. Foreign companies controlled the economy, so a powerful, privileged upper class did not develop. The peasants had not lost their lands, so they were less willing to form an exploited class that threatened those in power. Also, Honduras's vast banana industry was not labor-intensive, so the banana companies could afford to pay their workers relatively higher wages. In addition, the labor movement was strong, though labor unions were not officially legal until the 1950s, and the companies were more willing to grant concessions than companies in more labor-intensive industries.

Beginning in 1922, however, the Honduran military began to become stronger and more centralized. In that year, with the assistance of the U.S., an air force was created. In 1934 the School of Military Aviation was established; it was run by U.S. commanders until 1947. A Basic Arms School was founded in 1950, and officers were sent for further training to Panama. Though no organized guerrilla movement existed in Honduras at this time, this military buildup was designed primarily for counterinsurgency warfare. In the thick of the Cold War, any signs of labor unrest were attributed to communist agitators, and in the U.S. there was a great fear of communism gaining strength in Central America.

As it grew in size and power, the army began to play a larger role in government. Not until the early 1980s, however, did the military become especially repressive. Bordering both El Salvador and Nicaragua, Honduras was an ideal place for the Reagan administration's base of operations in the wars in these two countries. In 1988, for example, some 3200 U.S. troops were sent to Honduras after reports that Nicaraguan forces had crossed the Honduran border. In exchange for Honduras's cooperation as a base for U.S. military involvement in El Salvador and Nicaragua, the United States has increased military and economic aid to the country. One result of the military aid has been the emergence of death squads, formerly unknown to Honduras, and the strengthening of the military's control of the government. The infusion of economic aid has done little to raise the standard of living, and Honduras remains the second-poorest country in the entire Western hemisphere.

with programs to change this situation emerged only with great difficulty. Only recently, in the last third of the last century, was a relatively significant consolidation of government power achieved. But the achievements had limited scope, for the majority of the Central American population have continued to be poor and illiterate. The restriction the power of the Roman Catholic Church meant the end of the old paternalism, so that personal links of protection (for example, the landowner who was the *padrino*, or godfather, of many of his workers' children) increasingly gave way to the anonymity of contractual relations.

The agricultural frontier also has been a permanent issue in Central American history. The mirage of immeasurable wealth drew those eager to make their fortunes; nevertheless, the harsh reality of the jungle, the climate, illness, and the wild mountains kept "the frontier" from ever becoming a "promised land." Economic penetration and development, especially on the Caribbean coast, has been a slow and gradual process.

Artistic creation, mainly literary, reflected this rural, stagnant, and polarized world. Alienation and "estrangement" have been typical in the life and work of Central America's great artists. The more profound, universal, and extraordinary the literary, musical, sculptural, or pictorial creation, the greater has been the artist's estrangement in his or her own land.

Colonial religious architecture and art represented a more authentic and less foreign expression because its production was more communal. What has survived the earthquakes, volcanic eruptions, floods, and pillage reveals a profound originality in materials and colors and forms — a result of the melding of the Spanish and indigenous cultures. Although apparently destroyed in the Spanish conquest, the indigenous gods and myths survived in the rites, ceremonies, and devotions of the people's religion. And in some sense the ancient deities have been converted by architecture and religious art into carriers of the people's own cultures.

Nonetheless, the effect of powerful European influences during the second half of the nineteenth century was almost to smother popular culture with its pre-Columbian and colonial roots. Scorned by the upper and middle classes, popular culture survived only in fiestas and religious practices. Thus submerged in the collective memory, the folklore barely survived and in many cases has disappeared.

An Imported Culture. During that late-nineteenth-century era, when a more secular society was developing, the Central American upper and merchant classes were captivated by the culturally exotic. They adorned their houses with chandeliers, mirrors, and marbles, while swans, trumpets, and Viennese waltzes crowned their parties and salon conversations. With fewer resources but the same tastes, the middle class copied the practices of the well-to-do. The governments of the era commissioned European architects, sculptors, and painters, who left their mark on buildings and monuments. Likewise, the governments permitted the sale and removal of Central American archaeological treasures, which soon graced the halls of the great U.S. and European museums and private collections. Meanwhile, authors in the folkloric genre guaranteed a touch of "good conscience." Their idyllic world of lush land and crystal streams hid amid colorful landscapes and tender sentiments the misery, exploitation, and discrimination of the vast majority.

After World War I, modern mass culture profoundly penetrated the Central American societies through the combined influence of the mass media and the accelerated process of urbanization and modernization. The old ruling class and the modern business elite substituted the New York stock market for that of London. At the same time they exchanged Paris for Miami as a cultural mecca. The middle classes drastically modified their customs and patterns of consumption, adopting a U.S. lifestyle as a model. The lower classes have been influenced as well, so that fiestas and religious practices have declined in popularity. It is no surprise, then, that new religious movements and the so-called electronic church have increasingly been able to undermine the traditional Roman Catholic influence.

Since the 1960s, urban development and modernization have led to an important flowering of culture. In theater, literature, music, painting, and sculpture, new horizons and means of expression have opened up. This blossoming cultural movement is significant, though not extensive in comparison to that of the great Latin American cities. The rich variety of influences,

EL SALVADOR

If Honduras cannot be understood without reference to bananas, El Salvador cannot be understood without reference to coffee. In the mid-nineteenth century, El Salvador was faced with a declining demand for its chief export, indigo. The small but powerful elite that controlled the indigo industry then turned to coffee as a potential new cash crop. However, the land most appropriate for growing coffee was held by groups of peasants in communal farms. The elite group resolved this situation by exercising control through the government. An 1856 law required each communal farm to devote two-thirds of its land to coffee. Those that did not — and the high cost of a transition to coffee meant that many did not — had their land confiscated. By the 1880s all communal farms were simply declared illegal. The coffee elite were responsible for one of the most unjust land ownership patterns in Latin America. To counter revolts by peasants following the confiscation of their land, a police force was created.

The Great Depression of the 1930s disrupted El Salvador's coffee plantation economy. To cover their losses, the coffee elite laid off some workers and lowered the wages of others. As a result, peasants began to organize, and by 1932, 10.5 percent of workers had joined the Regional Federation of Salvadoran Workers. One group of peasants, led by Augustín Farabundo Martí, staged a rebellion in January 1932. Martí, who had been captured before the rebellion began, was executed and the rebellion crushed. The army killed not only the several hundred peasants involved in the rebellion, but another 30,000 as well. Pleased with the army's effectiveness in controlling the peasants, the elite entrusted the army with more power in government, and until 1979 the country was run by a series of military dictators.

The last of these was General Carlos Humberto Romero. When he came to power, the church was starting to be perceived as a threat to military control. Progressive priests were educating their constituencies in a new way, reading the Bible and applying it to their situation of poverty and oppression. In the same month Romero came to power, a death squad threatened to execute all Jesuits for being communists, echoing a similar statement by Romero himself before becoming president. The especially repressive nature of Romero's government caused the Carter administration to cut off U.S. military aid to El Salvador.

The Sandinista victory in Nicaragua in July 1979 made the Carter administration uncomfortable about its lack of involvement in El Salvador. Fearing a "second Nicaragua" in El Salvador, the U.S. publicly denounced Romero in the hope that a more moderate element in the military would stage a coup. This hope became reality in October 1979 when a ruling group, or junta, was installed. While the presence of civilians as well as military officers in the junta signaled that the military might give up some control, this hope proved vain. A series of moderates came and went, and the military's control tightened. 1980 was a year of unparalleled bloodshed. An average of thirty-five Salvadorans were killed each day, some by the newly formed guerrilla opposition group, the Farabundo Martí National Liberation Front (FMLN), but most by the military and right-wing death squads. In March the archbishop of San Salvador, Oscar Romero, was murdered while saying Mass. He had become a public advocate for justice for El Salvador's oppressed, and therefore an enemy of the military. He has since been revered as a martyr and saint by the Salvadoran poor.

José Napoleón Duarte came to power in 1984 with a promise to clean up the death squads, negotiate with the FMLN for an end to the war, and make land reform a priority. He achieved little success in any of these areas, yet by the end of Duarte's term the U.S. had given El Salvador over $3 billion in military and economic aid, under the pretext that reforms were progressing and that El Salvador had to be protected from the "communism" that had infected Nicaragua.

The presidential election of 1989 was won by Alfredo Cristiani of the Arena Party, a new party created only a few years earlier by Roberto D'Aubuisson, a former Army intelligence officer. Known as El Salvador's far-right party, Arena also has the dubious distinction of having controlled a network of death squads at its founding. Although D'Aubuisson himself has denied any involvement with death squads, the circumstantial evidence to the contrary is strong. D'Aubuisson has even been accused of being present at the very meeting to plan the assassination of Archbishop Romero. More recently, D'Aubuisson has been accused of using Cristiani, a man with no previous political experience, as his puppet. The U.S. government is putting its faith in Cristiani and Arena, and on President Bush's request the Congress recently passed the largest military and economic aid bill ever for El Salvador.

While governments, the military, and the rich jockey for power in El Salvador, the poor remain the victims, with little say in the power game being played at their expense. Remembering the witness of Archbishop Romero and others killed for their defense, the people have found it possible to hope in the midst of their mourning.

experiences, and productions reveals a deep national identity crisis, an incessant, anguished search for our own values.

Regional Unity and Diversity

The Peoples of the Pacific Coast and Central Highlands. In the highlands of Guatemala, a pre-Columbian and colonial world of the Maya and the Quiche indigenous peoples survives, with a diversity of languages and ethnic groups. It is a world unified by a common culture, similar community organizations, and a robust religious syncretism.[2]   But in the rest of Central America, with some exception for the Caribbean coast, all that remains of the Central American indigenous population are some wretched villages, despised, neglected, disintegrating.

In the strict sense, the majority of these groups can no longer be called "indigenous," since they long ago lost their own authentic characteristics. Their indigenous heritage is reflected in traditional crafts, food, festivals, and internal organization. Even many of these features are more colonial than properly indigenous.

Along the Pacific coastline, from southern Guatemala to northern Costa Rica, as in the central highlands of Honduras and El Salvador, the change is striking.   This is a "mestizo" Central America, people of mixed European and indigenous ancestry, in whose features the influence of African ancestry can also be noted. From agricultural practices to style of dress, daily life is determined by a common peasant culture. But nothing remains of the indigenous community, and the people's bond to the land has been drastically disrupted, especially because of the increasing influence of international agricultural export firms.

The human landscape is almost invariable: barefoot peasants wearing sombreros and with machetes at their belts; women carrying bundles or water jugs on their heads; naked children with swollen bellies. During the harvest season, trucks are filled with coffee, sugar cane, cotton, or large contingents of "cutters." The markets, bus terminals, plazas are filled with this peasant

---

[2]"Syncretism": A combination or reconciliation of diverse religious beliefs. For example, in Central America, Roman Catholic saints were substituted for and took on the characteristics of pre-Columbian gods. The festivals of the saints correspond in many ways to the rites of worship of these older deities.

presence, although here also are armed guards, under whose cloth-covered helmets the same mestizo or Negroid features can be seen.

The influence of the old Spanish culture is scarcely to be found among the urban middle and upper classes. The so-called second Europeanization, an immigration of business people and merchants mostly of Anglo-Saxon extraction in the last quarter of the nineteenth century, fed the coffee, railroad, and banana businesses. The immigrants markedly modified the habits of the middle and upper classes and erased much of the Spanish heritage. This new Europeanization was followed by the U.S. cultural influence.

In the highlands of Costa Rica, the physiognomy of mestizo Central America is somewhat different. The population is whiter and more homogeneous (genetically more European), while the Mesoamerican (Mayan and Mexican) cultural features are weaker. But peasant life has the same simplicity and crudeness, although it is true that more schools, fewer soldiers, and less poverty are to be seen.

The Peoples of the Caribbean Coast. Along the Caribbean coast, from Belize to Costa Rica, Central America is kin to the Afro-American Caribbean. This is "black Central America." In the seething tropical forests or the miniworlds of the banana or cocoa plantations, the black and indigenous cultures vegetate or suffer in agony. They live subjugated to the power and scorn — or at best the neglect — of the rest of Central America.

A large part of the Caribbean coast region, particularly the Mosquitia,[3] has had a history of conflict since the beginning of the seventeenth century, although it remained practically unknown to the Spanish during the colonial era. The English occupied it, exploited its natural resources, and subdued the indigenous population, even creating the artificial Mosquito kingdom with its own minor kings in the service of the British crown.

The English had a friendly attitude toward the ethnic Miskitos, to whom they supplied tools, utensils, and firearms. Treated as allies and not as slaves or enemies, the Miskitos trusted in the generosity of the English. For nearly two centuries, they served

---

[3]See note above, p. 11.

NICARAGUA

Even before the Spanish arrived, the area comprising present-day Nicaragua was sparsely populated. An indigenous population of less than
150,000 lived mostly on the Caribbean coast or around Lakes Nicaragua
and Managua. The Spanish colonized most of the country in the 1700s
and 1800s; the British took control of a small portion of the Caribbean
coast. Most of the present population are *mestizos*, but a small Miskito
Indian population still lives in eastern Nicaragua, an area they share with
a small population of black Nicaraguans, descendants of slaves or immigrants from Jamaica.

Until the Somoza family consolidated political power in 1937, two
political parties dominated the history of independent Nicaragua. The
Conservatives represented the elite of the city of Granada, the Liberals
the elite of León. Eventually the parties compromised on the "neutral"
city of Managua, following the overthrow of William Walker, a U.S. adven-
turer with a peculiar role in Nicaraguan history. Walker went to Nicaragua
in 1856 with dreams of establishing a Central American military empire,
with an economy built by slave labor and a canal linking the Pacific with
the Caribbean. With the support of the Liberals and of a U.S. company
that ran a ferry service along the San Juan River and Lake Nicaragua,
Walker proclaimed himself president. A year later he was overthrown
and the Conservatives took control for the next thirty years.

In the twentieth century, the U.S. has exercised growing power in Nicaraguan politics. In 1912, the U.S. sent a hundred Marines to Nicaragua,
ostensibly as embassy guards. When they were removed in 1925, civil
war broke out; they returned immediately, but as a force of several thousand. Meanwhile, the U.S. brokered a compromise between the Liberals
and the Conservatives.

One Liberal leader, Gen. Augusto César Sandino, refused to accept
this compromise and for the next six years fought a guerrilla war against
the Marines. To avoid the appearance of a U.S. war, the Marines created a Nicaraguan National Guard to fight Sandino's guerrillas. Popular
for his commitment to the poor, Sandino vowed to fight until the Marines
left, which they did in 1933. When Sandino then went to Managua to negotiate with the president, he was assassinated by order of the National
Guard commander, Anastasio Somoza García. Put in this command by
the Marines, Somoza ascended to political power. From 1936 to 1956,
Somoza was either president or the power behind puppet presidents.

After Somoza's death, his sons ruled Nicaragua for the next twenty-three years: Luis Somoza Debayle until his death in 1967 and Anastasio Somoza Debayle until 1979. The latter was especially ruthless and amassed a personal fortune worth half a billion dollars. When an earthquake in 1972 left thousands homeless in Managua, Somoza confiscated most of the relief aid and made no attempt to rebuild the city.

The Somozas were able to retain control for two reasons. First, they commanded the National Guard, which kept the people from protesting their oppression. Groups of peasants were massacred and individuals regularly executed. Second, the Somozas were masters at courting U.S. support. Educated in the U.S., they knew how to ingratiate themselves with U.S. diplomats and visitors. They faithfully supported U.S. anti-communist policies, even volunteering to send Nicaraguan troops to fight in Korea and Vietnam and allowing the 1961 Bay of Pigs invasion to be launched from Nicaragua.

The Somoza dynasty's repressiveness heightened the intensity of the movement to overthrow it. Led by the Sandinista Front for National Liberation (FSLN), the revolution brought together peasants, labor unions, students, the business community, the church. The small Sandinista army led the guerrilla resistance and the masses resisted nonviolently through strikes and other public protests. Named after Sandino, the Sandinistas faced massive problems after overthrowing Somoza in 1979, but they made considerable advances in health care, land reform, and literacy, holding a national campaign that reduced the illiteracy rate from 52 to 13 percent.

But the revolution quickly encountered a major threat. Former National Guard members who had fled to Honduras began conducting guerrilla activities inside Nicaragua. Ronald Reagan, newly elected president of the U.S., perceived the Sandinista revolution as a sign of communist influence and vowed to oppose it. With U.S. encouragement, former National Guard members, plus others disenchanted by the revolution, were recruited and formed into an army of counterrevolutionaries, or Contras, by the CIA. While the U.S. cut off all aid and imposed a trade embargo on Nicaragua on the economic front, the Contras fought in the countryside. Designed to destabilize the country, the fighting targeted hospitals, schools, roads and electric lines; accounts of kidnappings, torture, rape, and mass murder have abounded.

The Sandinista government's desire to revolutionize the entire society through education and economic justice has lost intensity because the war has demanded attention and money, some supplied by European and communist nations. It remains to be seen if Nicaragua will be left to decide its own future.

British military interests, attacking Spanish cities bordering on the Mosquitia. But they also subdued the other indigenous peoples of the Mosquitia, and even those of Panama. These populations were obligated to pay tribute to the Miskitos and, on occasion, their men were taken prisoners to be sold as slaves to pirates or English slave traders. Over time, the Miskitos' dominance was also expressed in disdain toward and discrimination against other indigenous cultures of the Caribbean region.

During the same era the region was a shelter for black people, who arrived as fugitives, victims of shipwreck, or slaves of English or Spanish pirates, merchants, and planters. Black immigration was strongly influenced by the intensification of English mining, timber, and commercial operations until the end of the eighteenth century in the Mosquitia, and thereafter in Belize (then British Honduras). The English preferred black to indigenous slaves, reserving for the indigenous people the role of strategic allies in their struggle against the Spanish crown.

At any rate, there resulted a great *mestizaje*, or mixing of races and cultures, evidenced in the pronounced black African features seen in the majority of the people native to the region. The profound process of cultural syncretism[4] is evident in the Afro-Caribbean influence on indigenous languages. Moreover, the continued immigration from the Caribbean reinforced Afro-Caribbean cultural patterns among the black residents of the coast. This interaction of values, customs, and traditions led to the cultural formation of the "black Creoles."

In the nineteenth century, U.S. economic, political, and military expansion in the Caribbean and Central America began to displace English control. The U.S. was most interested in a transoceanic route, natural resources, and the strategic value of the coasts. Bankers, business people, politicians, and real estate speculators invested aggressively throughout the whole Caribbean region, with the exception of Belize. Taking advantage of the area's "Anglophile" heritage, the North Americans developed large enterprises at a dizzying rate: timber, rubber, hides, minerals, railroads, bananas, and, most recently, fishing. The indigenous and black peoples were critical to these opera-

---

[4]See note above, p. 22.

tions and were thus introduced to a money economy based on salary and a pattern of high consumption.

Protestant missionaries — Anglican, Baptist, Methodist, and, especially, Moravian — provided religious support for the English colonial enterprise by promoting submission among the indigenous and black peoples and encouraging them in peaceful attitudes toward their oppressors. Later, the missionaries would help make available cheap labor for U.S. enterprises by favorably predisposing the black and indigenous peoples to salaried work and foreign customs.

The ecological system of river, jungle, and plain shaped the indigenous people's customs, economy, and entire way of life. This was the life to which people frequently returned after frustrating experiences as woodcutters, miners, or banana plantation workers. Faced with the pillage of their area's resources and the destruction of the environment, the indigenous people of the Caribbean region reacted almost instinctively by preserving the strength of community life, patterns of trade between groups, family ties, customs, tradition, and language. Of course, these characteristics — especially in the case of the Miskitos — were mixed with English, Afro-Caribbean, and U.S. influences, so the culture was quite variegated, but it kept an authentic seal of cultural unity in the midst of continuous change. The elderly and the women gave consistency and continuity to community life while the young men were away, and community became the only real security of these populations.

Two Histories in Conflict

This rich and tumultuous history had little impact on the rest of Central America. The great changes in mestizo Central America — at least until very recently — had little effect on the Caribbean region and its inhabitants. But these areas had not only two different histories — whose points of contact were the exception rather than the rule — but two histories in conflict. Both populations, the Caribbean region on the one hand and the central highlands and the Pacific coast on the other, developed resentment and discriminatory attitudes toward each other. They were also geographically isolated from one another. To travel to the Caribbean coast meant embarking on a tiring and

COSTA RICA

Unlike its neighbors to the northwest, Costa Rica does not suffer from a legacy of control by a small, economically powerful elite, large foreign corporations, or the military. Consequently, it has not experienced political and social unrest of the kind exhibited by peasants elsewhere in Central America. Its history has been relatively peaceful, without an armed insurgency, and, since 1948, Costa Rica has had no army at all.

After gaining its independence in 1838, Costa Rica was ruled by wealthy landowning families. Despite governing undemocratically, they were unusually attentive to the interests of the peasant majority. For example, dictator Braulio Carrillo (1835–42) actually distributed land to those who lived on it, increasing the already sizable number of small farmers. He encouraged the cultivation of coffee but established the industry as a small farm operation. This policy stood in sharp contrast to the confiscation of peasant land and destruction of the small communal farm system when coffee was introduced in El Salvador. To this day, Costa Rica's agriculture industry remains dependent on a large number of small farms.

The wealthy elite lost control of the country when Tomás Guardia became president (1870–82). Although a dictator, Guardia did not favor the rich but confiscated some of their property and exiled some of their leaders. He then opened Costa Rica to the cultivation of bananas by foreign companies. But unlike Honduras, in Costa Rica the banana companies were isolated geographically from most of the population and did not amass great influence in Costa Rica's government. At about the same time, an ambitious literacy program was launched. While Costa Rica's rulers had been benevolent in terms of land distribution, they showed little interest in education, and nearly 90 percent of the population was illiterate. The new literacy program helped pave the way for the institution of electoral democracy in 1889, which with few exceptions has remained Costa Rica's political system.

In the 1940s, Costa Rica's government began to extend its reach. President Rafael Calderón Guardia implemented the country's first labor laws and developed social security and public assistance programs. In 1948 Calderón was overthrown by a coalition of opponents and members of his own party. They objected to the support he was receiving from local communists and to his invalidation of an election won by an opposition candidate. After a brief civil war, the new government, led by acting president José Figueres, made even more substantial changes. Social programs were expanded, women given the right to vote, banks nationalized, and Roman Catholicism declared the official state religion. But the most amazing change was abolition of the military. The absence of an army has contributed to Costa Rica's peace and relative economic prosperity; in other Central American countries, repressive military systems have sapped much of the national incomes.

Costa Rica has found itself in the international limelight recently, primarily because of its president, Oscar Arias Sánchez. Taking a harder line against the Nicaraguan Contras than had his predecessor, he sought to remove their camps along the border with Nicaragua and to close down their office in Costa Rica, much against the wishes of the U.S. In February 1987 Arias met with representatives from Guatemala, El Salvador, Honduras, and Nicaragua to discuss regional peace proposals. He took the leading role in the ensuing process of working out a plan for peace in all the Central American countries. Six months later, the presidents of these countries again met in Esquipulas, Guatemala, and agreed to a peace plan largely devised by Arias. For this effort, Arias was awarded the Nobel Peace Prize.

The Arias plan proved an embarrassment to the Reagan administration: just days before, the administration had worked with a congressional leader, Democrat Jim Wright, to devise its own regional peace plan. The Arias plan not only upstaged the U.S. plan but also contradicted its emphasis on putting much of the blame for the region's instability on the Sandinistas. The Reagan administration saw the Arias plan as being too lenient on the Sandinistas. For standing up to the Reagan administration and initiating a Central American peace process developed by Central Americans themselves, Arias has been regarded as a strong leader committed to peace.

Despite Costa Rica's peaceful history and Arias's recent prestige, the country is showing signs of trouble. Under a severe economic crisis in the early 1980s, it cut back social services and sold public property to private corporations. Although this crisis has abated, the gap between rich and poor has widened, and the country has become more dependent on foreign capital. In addition to economic trouble, Costa Rica has experienced the new threat of militarization. In the 1980s the number of police doubled, and many of them have received military training, funded mostly with U.S. aid. Although it is difficult to predict whether Costa Rica can remain a peaceful nation without the enormous social problems of its neighbors, its history of fair land distribution and absence of violent social repression is a heritage worthy of pride.

dangerous journey of long overland travel on foot or horseback or by boat. And then there was the language barrier. Until very recently, Spanish was practically unknown to the majority of the black and indigenous peoples of the Caribbean region. The indigenous people, if they spoke anything besides their own languages, knew only a little "Creole-English" with Afro-Caribbean influences. Finally, there was a significant religious barrier. The Central highlands and Pacific were Catholic and the Caribbean coast was Protestant.

Because of their enormous ignorance of the ways of life, traditions, and social structure of the black and indigenous populations of the Caribbean region, plus racial and religious prejudices, the inhabitants of the central highlands and Pacific coastline formed erroneous ideas and stereotypes about those populations. A corresponding ignorance and prejudice on the part of the black and indigenous peoples of the Caribbean coast led to enormous resentment, mistrust, and antipathy.

This helps us to understand why to this day it is so difficult to integrate the peoples of the Caribbean coast into the rest of Central America. This serious problem is yet to be resolved by the governments of Honduras, Nicaragua, and Costa Rica. Only the Sandinistas in Nicaragua, with their plan of autonomy for the Caribbean coast, have taken significant steps in this regard, although conflict still resulted and many difficulties remain.

Chapter 3

Society and Politics Since 1950

We now turn to a closer look at the setting in which the prophetic church has arisen in Central America. In this chapter we look especially at the economics and politics of the region in the decades following World War II. In the next chapters we will consider the situation of the church in the same period.

Reformism in Perspective

The Central American countries have only lately been linked to the international market. And their role in that market has been very clear: they are to be producers of food and raw materials for the industrialized countries and consumers of products manufactured in the industrialized countries.

So an important sector in each national economy has been organized around the production of exportable products. This has been an economic development "from outside," marked by ironclad dependence on the economies of the industrialized countries. This dependence and consequent vulnerability of the Central American economies have been aggravated by their reliance on one or two agricultural products that comprise between 60 and 90 percent of exports and, therefore, of national income. Moreover, foreign investors have tended to control the financing, transport, and other commercial aspects of national production.

The introduction of bananas as an export crop in the late nineteenth and early twentieth centuries put a damper on modernization. This self-sufficient sector acted as its own empire, totally unintegrated into the national economies. The banana companies had autonomous power in their territories. The banana growers' total control of the railroads and the imposition of discriminatory tariffs that discouraged local development, the reduction in the amount of available land, and the siphoning off of profits all depressed the emerging national economies.

A new era seemed to open up at the end of the World War II. Underdevelopment and social problems were on everyone's agenda, and various reformist[1] plans were worked out.

In the social arena, the reformist issues were social service programs, the right to unionize, and the adoption of labor legislation. In the economic area, the gains included a certain amount of government control over banking and credit (as over against complete control by the ruling elites), agrarian reform, and a policy of economic diversification. In the political realm, respect for constitutional government and suffrage were called for, along with representative democracy and such nationalist goals as financial controls on the banana companies.

The relative success or failure of these reformist projects depended on three factors. In the first place, there was the degree to which the ruling classes were able to prevent change; in the cold war atmosphere, they labelled even the most timid reforms as communist as a way to discredit them. Second, there was the role of the middle class, their control of political power, and the degree to which they could appeal to a broader social base. And third, there was the impact of U.S. policy toward the region; the goal of that policy was the defense of U.S. economic, political, and military interests.

After a period of conflict, the groups in power finally accepted some reforms. These, however, amounted more to formal pronouncements than to real changes in-the power relationships. Nonetheless, the mere existence of certain laws and institutions provided a little room for social and political gains, which increased people's political awareness and led to more developed forms of political organization and social struggle.

The Postwar Boom in Agricultural Exports

Around 1950 a robust economy of agricultural and beef export was consolidated in all the countries of the region. Coffee and banana production was already receiving special attention and had developed advanced technology. But there were important

---

[1]"Reformism," as we shall see in more detail below, refers to various programs and proposals for economic development and political democratization that do not address the underlying structural causes of injustice. The Alliance for Progress falls within this category.

developments in cattle raising and in the production of cotton (which by 1955 displaced coffee as the principal export product in Nicaragua), as well as sugar, rice, and cocoa.

The large banana companies slowly abandoned their plantations in Guatemala and reduced their land under cultivation in Honduras and Costa Rica, where they held 20 percent of the arable land. But they extended their activities into cocoa, hemp, and African palm (in Costa Rica and Guatemala), and into cotton and sugar cane (Guatemala), or became commercial intermediaries for small local producers.

This agricultural diversification of export crops throughout Central America displaced the cultivation of basic grains needed for food to less favorable regions. It also deforested extensive areas of tropical woodland. Furthermore, it accentuated the concentration of land and agricultural production in the hands of wealthy landowners and outside investors. As more and more land that had been used for their own crops was taken over for export crops, the class of landless agricultural workers who were chronically underemployed grew larger. By the same token, this large-scale diversification consolidated a capitalist system of production in agriculture. It also led to an expansion of internal markets, which the Economic Commission for Latin America (CEPAL)[2] tried to use to promote industrial development.

A policy of regional integration developed through projects that crossed national boundaries. Toward the middle of the 1950s, CEPAL designed a Project of Economic Integration and Industrial Development. The CEPAL project recommended the development of a few selected industries in each country, in accordance with a regional plan that took into account each country's strengths and needs. The plan specified an important role for foreign capital but also stipulated that Central American investors maintain economic control.

The Counterrevolutionary Strategy of the 1960s

The Cuban Revolution in 1959 led the U.S. to shape a counterrevolutionary strategy for Latin America. The keys to this

---

[2]Comisión Económica para América Latina, an organ of the United Nations.

strategy were the Alliance for Progress[3] to stimulate economic development and the modernization and professionalization of national armed forces.

In the case of Central America, the Alliance imposed timid agrarian and tax reforms. It also encouraged "civilian" governments — where they were considered necessary — to provide a democratic façade for underlying military dictatorships. In this way, René Schick came to power in Nicaragua in 1963 and Julio César Méndez Montenegro in Guatemala in 1966.

The Alliance also brought credit "aid" to finance economic growth, which flowed principally through the U.S. Agency for International Development (AID), the Inter-American Development Bank (IDB), and the Central American Bank of Economic Integration. But, above all, it meant industrialization within the framework of the Central American Common Market, under the control of U.S. investors and U.S. agencies in the region.

The large landowners and others involved in exporting more traditional commodities did not renounce their privileges easily and therefore opposed the new tax and agrarian reforms. Because of their influence, in most of the countries the reforms advocated by the Alliance amounted to nothing more than relocating the rural population from "explosive zones" of grassroots unrest onto reservations, generally unsuitable for agriculture and without the most basic facilities for transport, communication, or credit. The foreign investors, local business people, and government workers saw the Alliance only in terms of their own economic advantage, as an easy way to enrich themselves.

The industrialization that accompanied the creation of the Central American Common Market substantially altered the economic and social complexion of the entire region. But the CEPAL project was reworked according to the interests of U.S. investors. A 1960 treaty created a free trade zone that significantly increased the potential of the national markets. Business

---

[3]The Alliance for Progress was established in 1961 by the Kennedy administration as a program for the economic development of Latin America (except Cuba). It was administered by the Inter-American Committee for the Alliance for Progress, a permanent committee within the Organization of American States. It included programs of development assistance and advocated land and tax reform.

among the Central American countries increased eightfold between 1961 and 1970. Seventy-five percent of its value was produced in U.S.-owned factories, or ones in which U.S. stockholders held the majority of shares.

Until 1969, U.S. investment in Central American manufacturing represented one-third of the total. Local investors were eager to invest their profits from agriculture and cattle in the new industries; other investors included Lebanese, Israeli, Syrian, German, and Italian business people. Economic control of the industrialization remained in the hands of foreign investors; local investors were simply junior partners, and most of the few existing industries were absorbed by the new monopolies. It is important to note, however, that the control and initiative assumed by foreign investors was due, in large part, to the inability of local landholding and commercial groups to become a true capitalist class, given their inclination to put their profits into, for example, real estate or foreign bank accounts rather than into new industries.

A modernization of government was required to create the conditions for a free enterprise system in a captive market; needed, for example, were legislation promoting industrial development, credit policies and tax exemptions for new economic activities, high tariff barriers, ceilings on pay raises, and ways to deter the labor movement. So the old ruling classes, which had been thrown into crisis by the Great Depression of 1929, were now completely dismantled and replaced by reformist governments. Increasingly, governments began to play a role in promoting economic growth, which meant greater government power, as well as higher foreign debt. Numerous government institutions were created to foster the new economic policies (for example, central banks, planning agencies), but also to try to cushion the growing social inequalities (for example, agencies for agrarian reform, housing, and health care).

Implementing this government reorganization was not easy. From the beginning, there were sharp disputes between the old coffee aristocracy, the new agricultural interests that emerged during the postwar period, the commercial sectors, and the new managerial class that now had close links to government. Since it was increasingly impossible for the different groups to co-

ordinate their interests through political parties, military governments (frequently with a constitutional basis) emerged as a
solution.

Landholders and business people delegated political power
to the military. Gradually, then, the armed forces took over
the governments and became the keystone of a new power
structure. The new era began in El Salvador in 1961 and in
Guatemala in 1963, while in Honduras the process took longer
(1971). The attempts of the Alliance for Progress to encourage
more democracy were placed on hold.

Following the example of their Nicaraguan colleagues in the
so-called Somoza Group, the military of the other Central American countries aspired to leave the ranks of simple "employ-
ees" of the economic elite and become "members" themselves.
From the 1960s on, the Somoza Group became the most important economic power of the region, controlling the Nicaraguan
media, airlines, plantations, factories, commercial distribution
centers, financial companies, hotels, and restaurants. Especially
during the 1970s, high-ranking Guatemalan, Salvadoran, and
Honduran military officers acquired a similar independent economic base.

Furthermore, the armed forces became for all practical purposes the strongest "political parties" of the region: for example, the Institutional Democratic party, which co-governed
in Guatemala for ten years; the National Conciliation, which
did the same in El Salvador from 1962 to 1979; and the
Somoza-controlled Liberal party in Nicaragua. During the 1960s
the Central American governments had more or less accepted
the rules of popular elections, but, now, under military control, they resorted to continual fraud — for example, the scan-
dalously rigged elections in El Salvador in 1972 and 1977, and
in Guatemala in 1974, 1978, and 1982.

The Price of Industrialization

Except in a few cases, no Central American country developed
economic programs that integrated industrial and agricultural
development, manufacturing finished goods from locally produced raw materials. Instead, industrialization was centered
in light or intermediate industries that depended on importing

semi-manufactured components to be assembled locally. This importing of more than 50 percent of the components of manufactured goods led to serious balance of trade problems; that is, the Central American countries owed more for what they imported than they earned from what they exported.

So the economies continued to be dependent on imports, and self-sufficient local industry did not develop. New jobs were not created at a rate that could absorb the rapid increase in population and the expulsion of farmworkers from the land due to foreign investment in agriculture. A class of factory workers was created, but it did not expand fast enough to absorb all the new urban population that needed jobs. In fact, the percentage of the economically active population employed in industry grew between 1950 and 1980 from 10 to only 20 percent.

Industrialization was also limited by the weak regional market, which, as we saw earlier, the various groups in power generally had no interest in widening. The most dynamic sectors of the economy absorbed most of the foreign investment. And the profits were not reinvested in Central America but taken abroad, while the production of consumer articles, of luxuries versus necessities, surpassed that of basic goods. In short, agriculture remained stagnant and the socioeconomic structure remained intact. Neither the kinds of changes in the class system that give rise to authentic economic development nor the consequent changes in property ownership occurred.

It was the poor majority who paid the price of industrialization. The benefits remained concentrated among a small group of business people and the middle-class sectors. In Costa Rica, greater government intervention and a consistent policy of reform toned down these effects considerably; but the price was a huge increase in public spending and foreign debt as well as a higher deficit in the balance of trade.

Industrialization accelerated the process of urbanization, and this in turn changed village sleepiness and provincial thrift into modern urban unrest, with growing unemployment, inadequate housing and social services, and increased crime. The "metropolitan zones" grew with no planning whatsoever. New attitudes and customs radically altered the traditional social patterns of rural life, while grassroots political organizations and protest movements took on new and frequently explosive dimensions in the urban environment.

When the process of industrialization and economic integration began, not every country in the region had the same level of development. Honduras, especially, had a very inferior infrastructure of highways and electricity, and its agriculture, industry, and banking system were not well developed. These differences placed the less developed countries at a disadvantage, so that they "financed" with their agricultural production the industrial expansion of the more advanced countries. By the end of the 1960s, most industries were concentrated in the countries with greater population densities and lower salaries (Guatemala and El Salvador). Nicaragua and Costa Rica threatened to leave the Common Market but eventually received certain "guarantees" that allowed them to continue to pursue industrial growth.

Industrialization also provoked intense competition among similar enterprises located in different countries. By around 1968 all ability to coordinate regional development was gone. Local industry leaders pressed governments to impose quotas, fees, and restrictions on products coming from neighboring countries. The problem became most acute in Honduras, whose government, faced with growing protests from industrial and business leaders, refused to allow its economy to continue to be subordinate to those of its neighbors, particularly El Salvador. This was one of the principal causes of the "Soccer War" of 1969 — so called because it was sparked by a dispute between crowds at a soccer game between the two countries. At the outset the Salvadoran military and business community were confident of a resounding military triumph. When the predicted victory did not occur, a crisis was precipitated in the Central American Common Market, of which the Honduran withdrawal in 1971 was a sign.

The U.S. counterrevolutionary strategy for Central America clearly represented, at its beginning, an attempt to incorporate and, in a certain sense, to "buy off" the working class, inculcating it with middle-class values and new patterns of consumption. At first, the Central American Common Market attracted the attention of some large international corporations controlled by U.S. economic interests. But the strategy did not succeed in dissipating class conflict in the region, since, as we have seen, industrialization did not solve land ownership and unemployment problems, balances of payments gradually deteriorated, and, finally, the Common Market began to break up as a result of growing regional inequalities.

When the Central American market reached the limit of its expansion, the international corporations changed their way of doing business. They maintained their investments, but by the end of the 1960s they were making few new investments. Some subsidiaries suspended their operations.

During the 1970s, the Central American Common Market barely survived. The Trilateralist[4] strategies of the Carter administration attempted to revitalize it, but the Sandinista victory in Nicaragua and the seething Salvadoran and Guatemalan situations seriously undermined those efforts.

It is no surprise, then, that new groups with economic interests in Central America appeared during those years. First, there were those from the southern U.S. (the "Sun Belt"). These groups emerged in the post–World War II era and, until 1968, were junior members of economic interests in the U.S. Northeast. They invested heavily in hotels and tourism, as well as in gambling, drugs, night clubs, and other activities linked to organized crime. With the change in the balance of power that came with the election of Richard Nixon (a political representative of these new interests), these groups gained political influence. They came to Central America with the unconditional support of the Nixon administration and official U.S. government agencies.

Second, there were Cuban exile groups, mostly based in Miami. Deeply anticommunist, they collaborated as junior partners with the Sun Belt interests. They came to Central America with abundant financial resources and impressive experience in establishing night clubs, casinos, and drug rings.

Third, there were local groups, particularly military and government bureaucrats, who began to compete for investments, as

---

[4]The Trilateral Commission was made up of business and political leaders from the United States, Western Europe, and Japan. Its purpose was to assure worldwide economic and political dominance of its partners.

well as the Cuban exiles in Central America, closely linked to their Miami compatriots.

The New Hard Line During the 1970s

With the Common Market's failure as a model of economic growth, the growing belligerence of student and grassroots movements in the region, and new priorities defined by the Sun Belt and its allies, the Nixon administration replaced the reformist strategy of the preceding Democratic administrations with a hard-line strategy. In this way, it attempted to prevent the total collapse of the Central American economies without making basic economic and social reforms.

In tandem with the new alliance of private interests (Sun Belt, Cuban exiles, local groups), the Nixon administration officially promoted its new economic and political strategy, hoping to keep the national economies functioning while limiting the development of grassroots protest movements. International aid agencies, especially the U.S. Agency for International Development (USAID), played an important role in this plan.

From 1970 on, AID sent experts, created new institutions, promoted specific projects, "suggested" new legislation, and granted loans to the Central American Bank of Economic Integration for secondary loans to new enterprises. The new activities included agricultural development and diversification (especially with foreign investment); nontraditional exports (agricultural and industrial), which reinforced the foreign influence on the economies of these countries; tourism; and mining (aluminum in Costa Rica, copper in Guatemala).

These highly profitable ventures were in the hands of a tiny group of private investors and were oriented toward the world market, not toward Central America. The region was used simply as a base of operations, an arrangement that required no structural reforms (in land use or financial policies, for example).

New exports, in particular, were promoted as the great panacea for the economic difficulties of Central America. The keystone of this policy was the incorporation of agriculture into the world market. The so-called green revolution — tremendous increases in cereal grain production through cultivation of new hybrid strains — was heralded as the future of the region.

But the highly acclaimed growth in export industries turned out to mean nothing more than setting up runaway shops, that is, production sites that move from the industrialized countries to regions with lower wages and weaker labor organizations. Raw materials were imported, processed, and then exported through the free trade zone of Colón in Panama. The green revolution turned out to be the "trick of the century," since it simply provided new opportunities for profit by transnational companies engaged in the storage and marketing of foodstuffs.

At the local level, the principal beneficiaries of U.S. aid were the large landholders, who increased their monopoly over the best lands. And since profits were higher in foreign markets, local production of basic foods declined, forcing more rural people into the cities.

The expansion of influence of the Sun Belt and its Miami allies was helped by their new political importance in the U.S., but also by the traditional investors' loss of interest in the region. The Cuban exiles also acquired considerable economic power: some as local executives of important U.S. subsidiaries, others as managers in the investment and finance sectors. They were also used as police reinforcements or recruits for government "dirty tricks" — especially in Guatemala — and some even achieved fairly significant political roles.

Unlike the reformism of the 1960s, this heavy-handed strategy had no intention of winning over or "buying off" the working class. It worked openly to subjugate it through an improved system for counterinsurgency and repression. Thus, any kind of truly democratic institutions virtually disappeared or at least were riddled with corruption.

The Sun Belt influence declined after Watergate and the 1976 U.S. election. The Carter administration withdrew U.S. support for military regimes and for clandestine operations. It even encouraged limited democracies and more equitable redistribution of wealth. Economically, it opted for a flexible strategy to reaffirm Latin American confidence in the free enterprise system. It promoted a growth model that followed guidelines set by the International Monetary Fund and attempted to strengthen the Central American Common Market and other Latin America economic pacts.

But a convergence of several factors led to the rapid failure of this plan: (1) a challenging of the economic privileges of the U.S. by its Trilateralist partners (Western Europe and Japan); (2) the inability of the Trilateralist countries to negotiate with the Organization of Petroleum Exporting Countries (OPEC); and (3) renewed third-world attempts to establish a "new international economic order."

Within the U.S., the recession of the late 1970s contributed another major factor, with unemployment, rampant inflation, balance of payment deficits, and declining productivity. There were also sharp contradictions between the interests of national and international investors. These discrepancies explain, for example, the hue and cry over the signing of the Panama Canal Treaties, as well as the disagreements within the Carter administration with regard to Latin American dictators.

As for Latin America, the endemic economic and organizational problems impeded economic development. The Trilateral proposal for "global development" (in which the third-world countries would simply produce industrial components and parts) was resisted by the most advanced countries (Brazil, Argentina, Mexico), who considered the proposal in conflict with their regional interests and aspirations.

There were also important political factors. One was the growing influence of socialist parties in Latin America. Another was the unmasking of the "new morality" of concern for human rights as a mere propaganda ploy that went no further than diplomatic pressure. But the most important obstacles to democracy in Latin America were factionalism and the lack of leadership and effective organization among the political groups in the majority of the countries.

Implications of Economic Growth

The postwar agricultural boom, the industrialization of the 1960s, and the promotion of nontraditional exports of the 1970s left a deep mark on the economic structure of the region.

The Central American economies experienced a growth rate previously unknown, shown by increases in the countries' Gross National Products. At the end of the 1970s the production per person was 80 percent greater than in 1950, even though population growth during the same period was one of the highest in the world. At the same time income and wealth became more highly concentrated in the hands of fewer people. The service and business sectors experienced significant expansion. Government resources were used to create a broad infrastructural network (highways, airports, dams, electrical power plants) to meet the demands of the foreign companies.

A complete transformation of the complexion of the class and social structure had also occurred. In El Salvador and Nicaragua, the old landowning aristocracy was integrated into a new entrepreneurial class that controlled industry and finance. In Costa Rica, by contrast, sectors involved in agricultural exports joined the old coffee aristocracy, while industrial and financial management classes developed separately. We also see the rise of a new kind of government and military power base, because governments had strengthened their means of control and the armed forces had consolidated their power. In Costa Rica, this new bureaucracy was almost exclusively political, while in the other Central American countries it was predominantly military.

The middle classes grew according to the pace of economic growth in each country. Technocrats acquired particular importance in government as well as in the new industrial and financial enterprises. A small class of blue-collar workers emerged, and the new class of landless rural workers grew. As foreign investment in agriculture increased, more and more of the rural population became landless workers for hire.

Finally, both in rural and urban areas, huge contingents of unemployed and underemployed people swelled the ranks of the poor in and around the principal cities.

Rebirth of the Grassroots Movements

Because of the impact of the Cuban revolution, but also because of the increasing influence of Marxist theory and the winds of renewal that stirred the sleeping consciousness of Christians after the critical papacy of John XXIII, a remarkable growth of grassroots movements occurred in the 1960s. The ruling class in Central America began to hear rumblings of protest.

The first to organize around more radical positions were middle-class intellectuals. Some helped organize guerrilla movements or participated in student revolts. In these years we also see university reform movements, the rise of a new generation of revolutionary intellectuals (musicians, poets, writers), and the founding of leftist political parties.

The appearance of guerrilla movements introduced a new ingredient to the balance of political forces in some countries of the region, producing new perspectives on social change. But during the 1960s, the romantic and even heroic actions of the guerrillas were not enough to motivate the rural population to revolt. The counterinsurgency strategy inaugurated under the auspices of the Alliance for Progress, which had helped equip and modernize the armed forces and police, allowed for efficient repression and successful antiguerrilla campaigns. By the end of the 1960s, the guerrillas were virtually defeated in Guatemala and Nicaragua and appeared to be controlled in El Salvador and Honduras.

But toward the middle of the 1970s, the guerrilla movement achieved a solid popular base in Nicaragua and El Salvador, while in Guatemala it was extended to the indigenous highland population. The fall of the Somoza military dictatorship in 1979 in Nicaragua marked the culmination of this period. It was followed that same year by the military coup in El Salvador — a clear response, supported by the Carter administration, to the growing success of the grassroots movements among the people.

In the 1960s there were significant, although sporadic, signs of social discontent, such as strikes of construction and banana workers and takeovers of land by peasant groups. Student and mass demonstrations began in 1959 in Panama, around the problem of the canal enclave. Particularly important was the 1964 demonstration, which obliged the government of President Roberto Chiari to break diplomatic relations with the United States. Also important were the demonstrations in Guatemala in 1962, in Nicaragua between 1967 and 1969 in defense of political prisoners, and in Costa Rica in 1970 against the approval of contracts with the U.S. mining company ALCOA.

The response of the governments and the ruling classes to the pressures for social change was repression. The delegation of political power to the military increasingly became a requirement for survival for landholders and business interests, who stubbornly saw the hand of the "communists" behind every conflict. Studies by experts and official U.S. missions were unanimous regarding the need for profound reforms. Nonetheless, in U.S. centers of power political and military concerns, along with the interests of large businesses with influence in official Washington circles, outweighed the concern for reform, so that U.S. support for the repressive regimes of the region continued.

The reaction of the armed forces and the ruling classes was increasingly unified. The Central American Defense Council (CONDECA), with U.S. military advisors, played a fundamental role. CONDECA was the product of a treaty signed by the armed forces of Guatemala, Honduras, and Nicaragua in 1963. El Salvador joined in 1965, and Panama in 1973. Costa Rica, although its army was abolished in 1948, symbolically joined in 1966.

This tendency toward regional military unity also explains the role that the Somoza regime and the National Guard of Nicaragua were able to play as guardians and sustainers of the Central American socioeconomic and political order. They promoted the overthrow of progressive, or even mildly reformist, governments, smothered coups d'état, or favored the "election" of selected candidates, as in the cases of some Salvadoran and Guatemalan military officers. The Somoza regime's role was enhanced by the apparent solidity of its political and military power; the nationalist frictions between El Salvador and Honduras in the Soccer War[5]; and, finally, the struggle for Panamanian sovereignty over the canal during the military government of General Omar Torrijos, beginning in 1969. We can see, then, why the fall of the Somoza military dictatorship meant the weakening of all Central American governments' economic, social, and political power. An entire way of distributing wealth and promoting production, of doing politics and governing, entered into profound crisis.

The overall political context was one of highly restricted democracies. Elections were strictly controlled and involved scant opposition participation. Numerous frauds and "preemptive" coups d'état insured that, generally, there would be no

---

[5]See above, p. 38.

transfer of power to the opposition. When governments did change, it was in limited, safeguarded ways. With the exception of Costa Rica, only the Guatemalan elections of 1944 and 1950 and those of Honduras in 1957 involved a clean, unrestricted transfer of political power.

Nonetheless, even these limited steps toward democracy opened up some political space for struggle and expressions of opposition. The Alliance for Progress, the rejection of the traditional parties that supported dictators, and the appearance of "modern" political parties, all favored this process. The international links of these new Social Christian and Social Democratic parties allowed them to count on some international support that enabled them to denounce abuses.

The more the military-government system lost credibility and had to resort to repression, the more grassroots protest grew. In every country, official repression was all out of proportion to the size and strength of the protests. Clandestine paramilitary groups organized as death squads to terrorize those who protested. With official backing, a rural paramilitary network was created to control the rural population from within.

Advocates of moderate political positions were sometimes physically annihilated; in Guatemala the leaders of the non-Marxist Left, Manuel Colom Argueta and Alberto Fuente Mohr, were assassinated. Others were simply paralyzed by the use of terror; these tactics were generally used against the Christian Democrats or other small parties of social democratic orientation. The absence of channels for protest and opposition — political parties or labor unions — led to polarization and direct political confrontation with the system.

Toward the middle of the 1970s, signs that the military governments of El Salvador and Guatemala might be opening up to more democracy led to increased efforts by dissenters to organize and mobilize the people. In El Salvador, the teachers' strike of 1972 and the violent 1977 protests against electoral fraud further radicalized the people. In Guatemala, work stoppages intensified in 1976. Enormous grassroots protests occurred: among the miners of Ixtahuacán, the Kek-chie Indians of Panzos, and opponents of increases in the urban transit fare. In Nicaragua, meanwhile, a broad spectrum of opposition forces, including guerrilla forces, managed to regroup in 1977.

Toward the end of the decade, the traditional power structure's crisis of credibility, now expressed through violent and radical conflict, spread throughout Central America. The structural problems related to the distribution of wealth and the exclusion of broad sectors of the population from the consumer market and from the political system took their toll. Civil disobedience was organized and led by new political and military forces with revolutionary platforms. The rural and indigenous populations, together with factory workers and the urban poor, demonstrated this new political energy.

U.S. strategies in the region and the wave of government-backed repression certainly fanned the flames of protest. But, above all, it was the growing awareness on the part of those who had some power in the society that pushed dissent into rebellion. These groups were gaining a deep understanding of the direction and dimensions of the Central American social conflicts. Groups of progressive young government officials tried, though with little success, on various occasions to implement new reformist alternatives. University student movements contributed to the development of a critical awareness of national and regional problems, and so became active centers of opposition — which explains their conflicts with the ruling class. The student movements played a key role of support for grassroots movements through street demonstrations, propaganda, and other forms of agitation. And, of course, we cannot forget the Christians.

Chapter 4

The Church Until the Mid-1960s

Beginning about 1870, movements arose to make governments throughout Latin America more secular; they enacted anticlerical policies that limited the power of the Roman Catholic Church. The policies remained in force longer in Central America than they did elsewhere in Latin America because the Central American dictatorships established in the early 1930s continued to find them useful.

Especially in Guatemala and El Salvador, where the church owned vast properties, the consequences of the rupture with the secular governments were ruinous for the church. In other countries, where the economic power of the church was less, its privileges were more gradually suppressed, and new policies of freedom of worship that provided security to foreign Protestant business people and investors were declared. During this long period, the numbers of Catholic clergy declined considerably, and the gap between the number of priests and the growing population remains a problem.

The "Re-Christianizing" Stage

During the 1940s and 1950s, the Central American governments and ruling classes saw the usefulness of supporting, and being supported by, the institutional church, and thus began a rebuilding of the church-state relationship. The church thereafter could count on the freedom to carry out its ministry without interference, as well as on state aid in such forms as tax exemption, postal allowances, and assistance in building construction.

The church received special support for its anticommunist activities. In Central America, perhaps more than elsewhere in Latin America, anticommunism — during the Cold War, but as far back as 1932 in El Salvador — provided the church with an excellent base for renewed influence. Over the previous decades the Roman Catholic hierarchy had perceived the spread of Protestantism as a serious threat, but now bishops and priests turned to preaching and writing against "atheistic communism," identified as the great enemy of democracy, freedom, and religion.

This anticommunist crusade in some places revitalized Catholicism. It also sparked the animosity of progressive workers, peasants, students, and intellectuals, because such a crusade allowed for quick condemnation and repression of any grassroots organizing that challenged, even remotely, the interests of the ruling classes.

In any case, this crusade smoothed the way for the rebuilding of church-state relations. As we shall see, this relationship was further solidified within the context of "developmentalism."[1]

Both the scarcity of priests and the new church-state relationship led the Roman Catholic Church to undertake, beginning in the 1950s, a true missionary offensive with the goal of expanding its coverage to the most remote parts of the region. Pope Pius XII himself called on first world churches to contribute funds and religious personnel to strengthen the missionary endeavors of the Central American church.

In 1956, in accord with the guidelines issued by the recently created Latin American Bishops Council (CELAM),[2] the First Assembly of Central American Bishops was held. On this occasion, the bishops agreed to undertake a crusade of faith, inspired by the approach of "Catholic Action"[3] and linked to a dynamic missionary movement. After nearly a century of anticlerical "persecution," the Central American church saw the possibility of recovering its lost power, so that it is no surprise that it adopted the aggressive outreach that had developed elsewhere in Latin America.

But first it was necessary to gather the strayed sheep, regroup the flock, improve the quality of their religious education, and form a committed lay leadership. It was hoped that these means would guarantee the church's influence over the rural and urban populations as well as renewing the glory of and the degree

---

[1]See below, p. 65.

[2]Consejo Episcopal Latinoamericano.

[3]Catholic Action: various Catholic lay movements, of European origin, that spread to Latin America in the 1930s. They were especially strong among the upper classes and had as their goal a re-Christianization of society.

of participation in worship. This undoubtedly would project
an image of power and strength, so desirable for an institution
eager for prestige and recognition.

Especially in rural areas, the religious life of broad sectors of
the Central American population was influenced by traditional
religious practices, which included the rosary, novenas, feasts of
patron saints, and processions. But there was also a place for
special powers and spirits perceived as inexplicable and super-
natural. If God and Catholic ceremonies weren't effective, then
many resorted to the healer's potions or the witch's spells.

Religious education regarding the sacraments was totally ab-
sent. Given the scarcity of priests, Christian leadership and
power over the things of God rested with a few members of
the community: the prayer leader, the guardian or "owner" of
the statue of the town's patron saint. This kind of religious
experience led to conformity, fatalism, and passivity.

The Central American bishops hoped to transform this traditional religious piety into a Catholic militancy enriched by
doctrinal education and sounder sacramental practice, more in
accord with the bishops' conception of the Christian life. Such
a task required solid institutional organization at the national
level, which in turn required the necessary religious personnel.

Missionary Outreach

Beginning in the mid-1950s, the number of foreign priests and of
sisters and brothers belonging to religious orders increased considerably. Numerous parishes, dioceses, and, in remote areas,
special jurisdictions called apostolic vicariates were established.
Some religious orders returned after many years of absence; others arrived for the first time. So the majority of these pastoral
workers[4] came to the countries of Central America ignorant of
their recent history, unique characteristics, and traditional religious practices. They also came with a colonialist mentality and,
at least at first, many tried to transplant the religious practices,
the lifestyle, and the approaches to ministry of their countries
of origin. Frequently they were rejected by the people.

---

[4]*Agentes de pastoral:* priests, sisters, brothers, and specially trained laypeople responsible for establishing and supporting the Christian communities,
especially among the poor.

They considered atheistic communism as the principal enemy of Roman Catholicism and the "Christianization" of pagan Central America as the best way to eradicate it. Nonetheless, a significant contingent of these foreign priests, sisters, and brothers — inspired by a missionary spirit that combined proclamation of the gospel with the struggle against paganism, communism, and underdevelopment — was sent to remote areas and began to share intensely in the life of the poor.

Inspired by the experience of Honduran diocese of Choluteca in 1957,[5] the Central American bishops strongly promoted parish missions, a kind of "Catholic crusade" focused on the institutional church and the principal dogmas of faith. Beginning in 1959, a legion of experienced Spanish missionaries traveled throughout Central America preaching, hearing confessions, officiating at Mass, and organizing processions. The results of this Holy Mission were more pompous than permanent, for the campaigns produced no significant changes in either the thinking or the life of the people.

At the beginning of the 1960s, many of the Central American clergy, especially the diocesan priests, were elderly. A third of the diocesan priests and 93 percent of the members of religious orders were foreigners, many of them Spaniards. Because many of the religious orders, for example, the Jesuits and Salesians, were dedicated principally to education and few religious orders specialized in rural mission work, church work was concentrated in the cities, particularly the capitals. Except in Honduras and Nicaragua, the number of parishes, priests, brothers, and sisters, especially after 1953, grew faster than the population. Despite this increase, the limited number of parishes and pastoral workers and the huge area and population for whose care they were responsible meant that the real penetration of the Roman Catholic Church into the region was still very slight.[6]

In the early 1960s, the confraternity[7] was still the most widespread religious organization in Guatemala — although it was

---

[5]See below, p. 69.

[6]See Mario Monteforte, *Centro América: Subdesarrollo y dependencia* (Mexico City: Instituto de Investigaciones Sociales de la UNAM, 1972), vol. 2, pp. 235–236.

[7]*Cofradía*, or traditional religious association of laypeople.

also found in other countries — where it was an important element of group identity for the indigenous population. During these years, especially in rural areas, the church made great efforts to create pious devotional associations (Knights Adorers of the Most Blessed Sacrament, Knights of Christ the King, Legion of Mary). One of the principal goals was to restore the people's confidence in the church institution and in the pastoral workers. In this way, prayer leaders, members of the confraternities, and spiritual leaders of traditional religion began to receive religious training and more direct contact with the Bible.

In this task of improving the religious education of these future lay pastoral workers, the church encountered a problem: extensive illiteracy. So literacy programs were rapidly developed. At that time radio seemed to offer a means of reaching the most people with opportunities for learning and knowledge of the "things of God." These programs were the forerunner of the radio schools, which in the late 1960s played an enormous role in increasing the social and political awareness of the peasants, particularly in Honduras, El Salvador, and Nicaragua.

The Cuban "Scare"

When it became clear, around 1961, that the Cuban Revolution would be socialist, the Roman Catholic Church in Central America almost without reservation joined the opposition coalition that included the U.S. government and the armies and the most conservative sectors of Central America. In 1962 the Central American bishops met in Managua and declared that "in order to bring an end to Fidel Castro the union of many Latin American governments is necessary," seconding the U.S. government's desire to create a continental army. One month later, the regional armies founded CONDECA[8] and broadcast a declaration remarkably similar to that of the bishops.

But as we have seen (pp. 31ff.), the solutions sought in these years depended not only on a strong military, but on development and industrialization and on the political reforms needed to support them. So the need for missionary assistance and foreign aid was reaffirmed, as well as the importance of strength-

---

[8]See above, p. 45.

ening the church-state alliance. The international development agencies, like the governments and the more progressive sectors of the local ruling classes, supported the church's campaign. For its part, the church looked on alliance with these sectors, which were considered progressive, as the fulfillment of a religious duty to humanize society by fighting poverty, especially in the rural areas.

The Central American governments found themselves in a dilemma: influential elements of church leadership supported the church's traditional policies that opposed social change, yet the U.S. government was promoting reform. Nonetheless, especially after the encyclical *Pacem in Terris* of Pope John XXIII (1963), government leaders found in the papal encyclicals and the documents of Vatican Council II, which they acclaimed enthusiastically, a common ground for alliance with the church. Faced with the intent of many church leaders to again make the institutional church an omnipotent social force, however, the governments tried to keep some distance from the local churches, suggesting "cordial relations" and "mutual respect."

The crude and fanatical anticommunism of the Cold War era, however, did gain ground. This gave new life to an anticommunist approach to ministry that is still very much alive today among broad sectors of the clergy and bishops of the region. "Atheistic communism" was identified as the great enemy of freedom, democracy, and religion. And almost every bishop, at that time, would explicitly condemn as "communist" any grassroots organization, not only those advocating revolution, but even those proposing modest reform.

All "good" Catholics therefore had to support the U.S. in order to overthrow the dangerous common enemy. Exaltation of the United States was personified in the figure of the Catholic president, John Kennedy. The Alliance for Progress was promoted with great enthusiasm by the church. Contributions of finances and personnel by U.S. Catholics were welcomed.

Among the Central American bishops there were some, like Bishop Evelio Domínguez in Honduras and Bishop Luis Chávez in El Salvador, who advocated a more positive approach to the "communist threat." They proposed confronting the advance of communism with committed social action on behalf of the most

impoverished people, in accord with Catholic Social Teaching.[9]
The Central American bishops did in fact establish various social service agencies (social secretariats, radio stations, broadcast
schools). Even some of the traditional religious organizations
began to deal with community problems (roads and bridges,
cooperatives, parish schools, medical dispensaries).

The governments, the most progressive ruling sectors, and
the international development agencies looked with sympathy
upon these initiatives and offered their support. As in many
other cases, the exception was Costa Rica. There the government itself was able to implement social service and community
development programs on behalf of the poor.

In urban areas, the church developed programs that sought
to win the political and economic elites, as well as the emerging middle class, back to Catholicism. Lay movements like
the Christian Family Movement and the Cursillo programs ap-
pealed to the elite, and specialized Catholic Action groups[10]
were strengthened among workers and students.

These movements were vital to that revival of Catholicism
sought by the bishops of Central America. In general, these
were movements professing individualistic Christian principles,
with little or no inclination to social action. Nonetheless, despite
their elitist character, many Catholics received through them,
especially the Catholic Action groups, training that later would
help them undertake political and even revolutionary activity.

This was, finally, the period of the founding of the Catholic universities by the Jesuits in Nicaragua, El Salvador, and
Guatemala. These universities were supported by governments
and industrial sectors of those countries, which hoped to train
professionals to participate in the fledgling process of Central
American economic integration.

In all these initiatives the Central American bishops were
trying to establish a significant church presence within the grassroots and student movements in order to forestall more radical

---

[9]"Catholic Social Teaching" refers to official Catholic Church teaching on
the relationship between church and society. Its highlights include the papal
encyclicals *Rerum Novarum* (1891), *Quadragesimo Anno* (1931), *Mater et Magistra* (1961), *Populorum Progressio* (1967), and statements of Vatican Council II.
[10]See note above, p. 49.

options based on class struggle. Confronted with growing acceptance of Marxist and socialist ideas by broad sectors of workers, students, and intellectuals, the bishops promoted Catholic Social Teaching as the only true solution to the grave social, economic, and political problems of Central America. Many middle-class laypeople became advocates of the study and dissemination of this teaching. The majority of these Catholics quickly moved into membership in the Christian Democratic parties founded during this period in Guatemala, El Salvador, and Honduras.

By the late 1960s, the influence of the institutional Catholic Church began to be felt in the Central American countries. This won it increasing respect from political, economic, and military powers. And now the impact of the Medellín "event" meant that the church could no longer isolate itself from the upheavals of Central American society as it had done during the difficult decades of rebuilding its prestige.

Chapter 5

The Medellín Event

At the landmark meeting of the Latin American bishops held in Medellín (pronounced *May-they-YEEN*), Colombia, in 1968, two major currents of the 1960s flowed together.

On the one hand, there were the great events and documents of the Catholic bishops, both on a worldwide and a Latin American level: the Second Vatican Council (1962–1965); the three great social encyclicals, *Mater et Magistra* (1961), *Pacem in Terris* (1963), *Populorum Progressio* (1967); the "Message of the Bishops of the Third World" (1967); the Tenth Assembly of the Latin American Bishops Conference (CELAM) in 1966 on the theme "Theological Reflection on Development"; and the meetings of various departments of CELAM — on Joint Pastoral Planning (1966), on Catholic Universities (1967), on Missions (1968), and on the Church and Social Change (1968).

On the other hand, there was the "Christian movement" arising from the grassroots of the Latin American churches. The universal significance and vitality of what happened at Medellín is due, in large measure, to the convergence of these two currents.[1]

Vatican Council II

The Second Vatican Council unleashed enormous changes in the life of the Roman Catholic Church worldwide. In the Latin American church, particularly in Central America, new theological emphases reshaped the church's practice.

1. *The gospel was redefined as action more than as doctrine.* According to the Council, emphasis must be placed on our way of life, that is, on how we participate in the building of God's Reign.

---

[1]See Pablo Richard, *La Iglesia latino-americana entre el temor y la esperanza: Apuntes teológicos para la década de los 80* (San José, Costa Rica: DEI, 1980), pp. 49–52.

2. *A new emphasis was given to history as the place where revelation occurs.* This represented a return to the true meaning of the Word of God, a living Word that continues to speak and act among human beings today, inviting them to creativity and struggle against the forces of death.

3. *The church was reinterpreted as the sacrament of salvation and as the People of God.* The church exists to serve the world, not the reverse. It exists to help establish the Reign of God. And the Reign of God is not the church, as had traditionally been taught, but rather a world in accord with the will of God, in which truth, justice, and love reign. The church's mission is evangelization, in which it announces the saving will of God as it seeks to bring God's will to reality in the humanization and total liberation of human beings. That mission is to be exercised in service and humility, not in an otherworldly, arrogant, or authoritarian way. The church is, above all, a community of sisters and brothers, of believers in Christ who serve the Reign of God, a community in which all can and should contribute their own gifts and service. The faith and hope that are given to all God's people take precedence over any particular gifts and ministries. The church is a community in which no one is greater than another. This means that the laity must abandon their status as "children" and exercise their ministries responsibly, that they must express their witness publicly. The bishops are to exercise authority as service, to listen, to discern holiness in the People of God, to resolve conflicts through dialogue rather than administratively.

4. *The priesthood was reinterpreted as ministry.* The priest is a servant of the gospel, a member of the People of God. Among the people, and with them, the priest exercises service, with a variety of gifts and tasks.

5. *There was a new conception of the world and its relationship to the church.* The world is no more a "vale of tears," but the positive creation of God. It is the place to live, to love, and to be free. The principal task of believers is to collaborate with God as creators to make this world a land of brothers and sisters.

Many of the Latin American bishops who attended the Second Vatican Council returned to their dioceses with a strong concern for church renewal, ready to turn their attention to the world and its problems. With the support of national bishops' commissions, departments of CELAM , and various training institutes, innovations in worship, religious education, and social action began to multiply.

Developmentalism, Dependency, Liberation

In accordance with the "developmentalist" theories[2] that prevailed at the time, many in the church saw the solution to problems of inequality and injustice in continuous development, financed by aid from the industrialized countries, with no questioning of the economic and political mechanisms that caused the injustice.

Since 1961, Cuba had demonstrated the possibility of establishing a socialist system in Latin America. At the same time, the liberation and guerrilla movements stimulated hope for a rapid and radical revolution. As an alternative to this "revolutionary temptation," there appeared in 1961, as we have seen, the U.S. counterrevolutionary strategy based on the Alliance for Progress, along with the "revolution in liberty" (1964) proposed in Chile by the Christian Democrats as an expression of Catholic Social Teaching.[3]

But the U.S. became increasingly discredited by the war in Vietnam and its problems of racial discrimination. Likewise, unlimited confidence in "development" was gradually replaced by disappointment in and rejection of "developmentalism." Meanwhile, the policies and repressive practices of the new type of military governments established in Brazil (1964) and Argentina (1966) posed new problems for more politically aware Christians. And tensions developed in the Central American countries that began to call into question the previous harmonious relations between the church hierarchy and the government ruling classes.

During these years, Latin American sociologists, economists, and political scientists began to propose a very different interpretation of "underdevelopment." This new theory of "dependency" explained the underdevelopment of the poor countries as the product of the development of the industrialized countries;

---

[2]See below, p. 65.
[3]See note above, p. 54.

that is, the industrialized countries become enriched and developed by impoverishing and underdeveloping the poor countries. This new point of view reinforced the struggle for liberation, which began to involve groups of laypeople and priests, among others.

Because of the success of the socialist revolution in Cuba and the failures of many plans to reform and "develop" their countries, Latin American grassroots movements had increasingly seen their situation as a struggle between classes, because they no longer believed reforms could bridge the gap between the "haves" and the "have-nots." The growth of these grassroots movements and the worsening conditions created by dependency both had a great impact upon the social and political consciousness of many Christians.

The economic and political crisis of the systems in power in Central America meant a crisis for the model of the "church of Christendom,"[4] which so strongly depended on these systems. Church social programs, Catholic movements and parties, the Catholic educational system and universities, Catholic Social Teaching, models of ministry — all entered into crisis. The first reaction came from the members of Catholic Action groups.[5] Then came increased political awareness among the grassroots and peasant organizations, with which a significant number of pastoral workers were involved. During these years in the mid-1960s, many Catholics began to be active in grassroots movements and in leftist parties, where they met and began to work with nonbelievers.

Groups of priests began to organize in various countries (ONIS in Peru, Priests for the Third World in Argentina, Golconda in Colombia). As church groups they took action and issued public position statements, regarding social and political problems.

Even before the Medellín conference, some Latin American Christians began to develop a theology that based its method and themes on the political commitment of Christians in the grassroots movements. An early but definitive formulation, "To-

---

[4]See note above, p. 6.
[5]See note above, p. 49.

ward a Theology of Liberation," was presented in July 1968
by Gustavo Gutiérrez, a priest from Lima, at a conference in
Chimbote, Peru.

The most dynamic and politically aware sectors of the church
pressed for the adoption of innovative political and pastoral approaches. This pressure welled up and overflowed at the Second
General Conference of Latin American Bishops, held August 26–
September 6, 1968, in the city of Medellín, Colombia.

The Renewal Unleashed by Medellín

In accord with the Vatican II insistence on looking at the world
and asking how God's plan is incarnated there, the Medellín
Conference looked at Latin American reality and found it rife
with poverty and injustice. It was no surprise, therefore, that
Medellín applied the teaching of Vatican II from the perspective
of the poor.

The bishops at Medellín characterized the Latin American
church as a church of the poor. In its mission to the world, the
church should take up as its own the cry of the poor and their
yearning for liberation, giving to both their ultimate meaning.
Within the church, the People of God should be conceived as the
people who are poor, who are all direct and privileged recipients
of the revelation and love of God.

This church of the poor makes its demands. It must denounce
poverty and analyze and unmask its structural causes; that is,
it must be a prophetic church. It must embody in itself the
poverty of the poor; that is, it must be an impoverished church
in solidarity with the poor. It must read the gospel with the
eyes of the poor. It must make clear the choice between the
idols of death and the true God of life, between an inadequate
doctrinal proclamation of the lordship of Christ and the true
following of Jesus. It must evangelize the poor and allow itself
to be evangelized by them. It must give priority to the poor
within the church and seek new communal forms of church life.
Finally, it must prepare itself for persecution and martyrdom,
which result inevitably from such commitments.

Social violence and injustice, as well as a widespread lack of
concern for the pain of the poorest, were considered by many
at Medellín as resounding proof of how little gospel values

had permeated the life of baptized Christians: Latin American Catholics had been "indoctrinated" but very inadequately "evangelized." On the basis of the Vatican Council's affirmation regarding the close link between doctrine and Christian life, emphasis began to be focused on faith concerned not so much with "correct teaching" ("orthodoxy") as with "correct action" ("orthopraxis"). This new evangelization required living communities in which the gospel could take root. And so the Christian base communities that were born during this period were affirmed at Medellín.[6] In them many gifts would flower, many ministries turn clearly toward society.

Many pastoral workers now found themselves in an "Exodus" condition. This new approach meant a geographical Exodus, because they had to move in order to live with the poor. It meant a social and human Exodus, because they had to change the old relationships that profoundly influenced their way of reading the gospel and reflecting on the faith. It meant an Exodus of the affections, because their affection was now for the poor, who became close friends and sisters and brothers. It meant an Exodus from work, because they had to learn new ways of working to make a living. It meant a cultural Exodus, because they had to live, adopt, and reflect upon new ways to understand the faith, to rediscover their roots in the land itself. Finally, it mean a spiritual Exodus, because their new life was a true and profound experience of the God of the poor.

As the Christian base communities grew in understanding their responsibility to build the Reign of God and to continue God's creative work, they increasingly dedicated themselves to justice, freedom, and peace. In this way was born a liberating "practice" that ends any split between faith and justice or faith and politics. Many Christians in the communities, with increasingly clear motivation based on their faith, began to participate in the growing grassroots movements. In this way, new relationships, which would renew the Latin American Roman Catholic Church, came into being. But at the same time, numerous conflicts developed.

The theology of liberation, developed by theologians atten-

---

[6]See note above, p. 8.

tive to the new experience of faith of the poor in their struggle against injustice, was nourished by this spiritual experience of the God of the poor. This innovative theological reflection attempted to understand the meaning of society and how God acts in our times. Its requirement of conversion to the poor and of commitment to total liberation often meant that ministry was oriented toward that liberation.

In summary, the Medellín "event" allowed for a new vision and interpretation of Latin America by many Christians. As awareness of injustice increased, they began to interpret their situation in terms of domination and colonialism, both internal and external. They began to analyze the structures of social and political injustice.

Although it is crucial, this shift is very hard to describe. Previously, many Latin American Christians had placed their hopes for society in convincing the powerful to allow those less powerful to benefit from various forms of development. But now they could begin to see the need for a radical change carried out by the oppressed themselves. Gradually the idea of liberation became the key to both ministry and theological reflection. By the same token, some bishops began to reconsider their traditional alliances with the government and the ruling classes. They began to distance themselves from those in power and place themselves closer to, or even among, the poor. Let us now look to see in more detail how the shift came about.

Chapter 6

The "Developmentalist" Transition in the Church

The period from 1965 to 1969 in Central America was one of transition from a church of Christendom to a prophetic church. The process moved to different rhythms in each country.

Repercussions of Vatican II

Because they belonged to international organizations, men and women who were members of Roman Catholic religious orders had more access than diocesan priests to the documents of Vatican Council II and were more likely to be inspired by the Council's spirit. Renewal affected these churchpeople more rapidly than others and we see among them a growing faith response to the challenge of poverty. Especially in the most remote dioceses, where most of the pastoral workers came from outside Central America, the task of *aggiornamento* (bringing up to date) of the Roman Catholic Church led to burgeoning activity: courses, meetings, radio schools, organizations of the clergy and other pastoral workers, and participation in nonchurch movements.

But in some parts of Central America, especially among the diocesan clergy, the effect of the Vatican Council was negligible or delayed. The clearest case is that of Costa Rica, where, it has been said, the effect of the Council was nothing more than "turning the altar around and saying Mass in Spanish."

There are various reasons for this slow response. First, many of the priests were elderly. Second, churches were not organized to communicate the important transformations occurring in the church worldwide. Third, some conservative bishops and clergy were opposed to making the conciliar documents known and putting them into practice — or did so half-heartedly. Fourth, church leadership, especially the native diocesan clergy, was isolated from progressive international study centers. And finally, the seminary training received by these clergy was inadequate:

otherworldly, disconnected from the real problems of their countries, and devoid of intellectual concern (producing priests who neither read, nor studied, nor asked questions).

Nonetheless, although very timidly and gradually in some cases, renewal managed to move beyond the changes in worship. New approaches to ministry were undertaken that, although they generally still did not address sociopolitical issues, did deal with creating a community spirit, with strengthening the role of the laity and of family life, and with overcoming sexism.

The case of El Salvador was very different. The open mind, intellectual acumen, and obedience to institutional direction that characterized the archbishop of San Salvador, Luis Chávez González, led him, as early as the late 1950s, to adopt some of the guidelines issued by the recently established Latin American Bishops Conference and to encourage intensive social action.

After Vatican II the archbishop issued numerous letters on social themes and encouraged various projects on behalf of the peasant organizations. Efforts were made to improve seminary education. Young seminarians and priests were sent abroad to study in theological schools and universities, and a group of outstanding professors and specialized church workers were trained. The archdiocesan clergy were well educated. This was very important, given the influence of the archdiocese of San Salvador on the rest of the Salvadoran church.

But on the whole the Central American Roman Catholic Church remained committed to development programs, still believing in their efficacy. And most of the bishops did not wish to jeopardize the church's good relationship with the power structure by calling for more justice.

Nonetheless, small groups of lay people and pastoral workers began to raise questions about the real causes of poverty, since poverty persisted and was even getting worse despite intense foreign aid and extensive development programs. In this regard, the influence of the Vatican II document *Gaudium et Spes* (Pastoral Constitution on the Church in the Modern World, 1965) was very important. But even more important was the papal encyclical of Pope Paul VI, *Populorum Progressio* (1967). In the climate of widespread unrest of those years, this teaching helped awaken the social conscience of many Catholics, who began to denounce the exploitation and oppression. There also were some attempts — hardly fruitful at the time — at dialogue between Christians and Marxists.

The Crusade Against Underdevelopment

By the late 1950s, the theory of developmentalism, disseminated by CEPAL[1] and other international agencies, began to make headway in the region. The premises of developmentalism were that the existing misery was the product of the backwardness of the Latin American societies and that it was possible to overcome the backwardness through modernization and technical progress. This theory relied on "progress" itself to overcome underdevelopment rather than on any reorganization of society or redistribution of wealth. Despite its erroneous premises, developmentalism helped awaken a greater social awareness as well as a sense of urgency to overcome the region's economic backwardness. Modernization and technological innovation were presented to the Central American governments as powerful imperatives.

Inspired by the new papal social encyclicals and the spirit of renewal of the Vatican Council, the Central American Catholic Church experienced its own renewal. It increasingly accepted responsibility for building a more just and humane society as well as for renewing its own institutions. It soon began to participate fully in the process of development. It relied on a theology of development, which baptized technical progress and with it capitalist modernization. Thus the struggle against underdevelopment took on religious significance.

The developmentalism developed by the Central American church recognized that a participatory society, that is, one where all people can influence political, economic, and social life, is the opposite of a society where some people are marginated and have no possibility for any significant participation. Church leaders believed that social action programs advocated by CELAM in 1966 would reconcile these two poles and would integrate the marginalized people into society. Through

---

[1]See note, above, p. 33.

planned development of grassroots organizations, the people could achieve true development; they would be the beneficiaries of economic and technical development.

This kind of belief increased the church's commitment to improve the society, but it was a commitment very much under the sway of secular developmentalist theory and it ignored the real social conflicts. It considered technical progress as the "engine of development," but could not see the real mechanisms that excluded the poor from the benefits of technology. Therefore it functioned perfectly well for the emerging business classes, as well as for the foreign investors who were expanding capitalism in the region.

So we can say that in the 1965–1969 period a movement based on Catholic Social Teaching[2] that combined church programs and grassroots organizations rallied around the theory of developmentalism. It was a period of great activity in which pastoral workers, lay social action agencies, and peasant organizations sought common means to attack the poverty and underdevelopment of the Central American people.

Especially in Guatemala, El Salvador, and Honduras, social development programs penetrated every area of church activity. During this period the church built schools, roads, dispensaries, and parish clinics and it organized cooperatives and peasant associations. This was no longer a simple anticommunist crusade, but rather a crusade against underdevelopment, and its principal leaders were expatriate pastoral workers.

Because of the broadening parish and institutional network, the efforts of the pastoral workers had significant impact. And the people themselves were not indifferent spectators; they actively persuaded other Catholics to participate in development projects. Members of the old religious organizations, leaders in the radio schools, and workshop graduates were rapidly integrated into peasant and community organizations.

In some countries Caritas, the Catholic relief agency, was reorganized. Emphasis was now placed on development projects rather than on traditional forms of aid. Specialists in social ministry were brought in to train leaders and provide techni-

[2]See above, p. 54.

cal advice. Abundant foreign financial aid also assisted Catholic communications media (radio stations, newspapers, publishing houses). The radio schools, particularly, received strong support. Literacy training was linked with understanding national and regional problems and with community social action.

In Honduras, educational work began to be carried out from a religious point of view. The radio schools had been based on a secular model of education. But the growth of the "Celebration of the Word of God" program in the diocese of Choluteca in 1966 provided a new model of education in worship and doctrine. This program, which rapidly spread to neighboring countries, encouraged the participation of lay people in worship activity formerly reserved for priests. This in turn fostered religious education in gospel values within the heart of the Christian community.

International aid also promoted the growth of rural training centers ("El Castaño" in El Salvador, "La Colmena" in Honduras, "San Benito" in Guatemala, and the Capuchin Fathers' center in Zelaya, Nicaragua, among others). The pioneers of these experiments in ministry were also for the most part foreign pastoral workers. These centers sought to educate rural leaders who would then organize development projects within their own communities. They were given instruction in religion, agriculture, cooperatives, community development, hygiene, and health. The graduates — for whom the centers provided "follow-up" — began to have an impact in their communities, first in agriculture and religion, and later in politics. So a vanguard of Christian leadership grew up, able to apply their training to secular organizations as well as in the church, where they continued to find strength in biblical reflection, religious practice, and the sense of Christian community.

By beginning with the Word of God, reflected upon in relation to daily events during the Bible studies, the community Mass, or the Celebration of the Word, many Central American Catholics grew in their commitment to participate in development projects. Throughout this process, various secular educational and organizational institutions (cooperatives, radio schools, peasant associations), generally under church supervision, helped prepare people for the activities undertaken. In this way, many people began a slow process of "conscientiza-tion," that is, a growing political awareness and commitment that, during the 1970s, would result in the formation of the first Christian base communities.

Most of the institutional Roman Catholic Church in Central America gave some support to church developmentalism as a so-lution to the challenges of poverty. Of course, significant sectors of the church looked askance at this interest in social action, be-lieving that it distorted the true mission of the church, and they refused to participate.

Pioneer Experiments in Ministry

Some particularly important pioneering experiments interested the most energetic pastoral workers, many of whom participated in these experiments for their own education. These experi-ments became known throughout Central America.

Two Parishes in Panama. In the parish of Santa Fe in the Panamanian diocese of Veraguas, the Colombian priest Héctor Gallegos led developmentalist projects from 1968 on. Coopera-tives and training programs for peasant leaders were organized throughout the diocese by his John XXIII Center.

Gallegos encouraged self-help agricultural programs based on cooperative work and designed to achieve economic indepen-dence for the peasants. He also created a network of Christian communities that began to read the Bible from the point of view of the struggle for justice. Eventually this kind of outlook led the peasants to rethink their situation in more radical ways and to break with the center's developmentalist approach.

The program was attacked by the landlords of the area, and in 1971 Gallegos was kidnapped and murdered, making him the first martyr priest of the region. The experience of the Santa Fe parish came to have great symbolic value for all of Central America.

San Miguelito was a slum that grew up in Panama City dur-ing the 1950s. In 1963, three U.S. priests arrived, who initiated a plan that linked the struggle for well-being (material, personal, and social) to the proclamation of the gospel as a liberating message of human dignity and community. As a result the peo-ple organized to struggle for social justice. A network of small

Christian communities called the "Family of God" arose. So before Christian base communities were even heard of, Catholics were gathering here for Bible reading, reflection on their situation, and Christian education.

A training center for grassroots leaders, MUNDO (Movement for National Unification, Development, and Orientation) was founded. It was independent of the parish to avoid the risk of excessive clerical influence on political action. An institute was also established for theological training of pastoral workers. Pastoral workers from Nicaragua, Guatemala, and El Salvador who attended the institute's courses learned basic principles that they could apply later in their own settings.

A Diocese in Honduras. In the diocese of Choluteca, Honduras, an innovative experiment in ministry gave rise to the Celebration of the Word of God program and had great influence in Nicaragua and El Salvador.

Members of a Canadian religious order, the Xaverians, took charge of the Choluteca diocese in 1955. In 1959, they carried out a large "mission," a parish church renewal program, which enabled them to identify laypeople with talents for organizing their communities. The scarcity of priests and nuns quickly made it necessary to incorporate these peasant leaders into pastoral work.

Beginning in the early 1960s, social development projects were organized. Radio schools provided technical training in agriculture and community organization. The local radio school leaders were in charge of adapting the messages to their communities. Homemakers clubs enabled women to participate in community life. "Celebrators of the Word" were trained to supplement the priests in an innovative type of Sunday celebration based on reading and discussing the Bible. This model of training proved very effective and quickly spread to Nicaragua and El Salvador.

In Choluteca as in other areas, re-reading the Bible from a liberation perspective with local lay leadership amid the people's actual experiences of poverty and exploitation led communities to organize themselves for action. In this way, the Christian communities became part of (or even originated) intense peasant struggles in the early 1970s in central and southern Honduras.

Methods. The method common to all these pioneering experiments was for people to analyze their own situation and judge it in the light of faith, in order to transform it. And this approach spread rapidly to other experiments in Central America. In every case, the first great discovery that the lay people together with their priests and sisters made was that their faith, their church, meant *community*, and how this kind of community could come to life in their own situations.

The members of those fledgling Christian base communities began to interpret the Bible, to give Sunday sermons, to lead in evangelization efforts, including composing music and lyrics for their own Masses. Members of the parish of St. Paul the Apostle in Managua, for example, composed the text and music for their own Mass, recorded in 1969 as the "Nicaraguan People's Mass" (*Misa Popular Nicaragüense*). Distribution of the records was later prohibited by the bishops, who considered the Mass subversive.

Some of the Nicaraguan experiments in ministry, like those in Panama and Honduras, created a strong missionary spirit that led them to share their experience with the Catholics of other neighborhoods and towns. This was the case of the parish of St. Paul the Apostle, whose influence was felt not only in other parishes of the archdiocese of Managua, but also on the Nicaraguan Caribbean coast. The same occurred with "La Zacamil" in El Salvador.

Among the important experiences of this period were the ministries developed in some of the Catholic schools, mostly private schools in urban areas. The growing awareness of injustice and exploitation in Central America led members of religious orders, who were the teachers in those schools, to a real identity crisis. They began to question the very reasons for the existence of schools attended by the children of the privileged class, while the poor majority were almost abandoned. The most aware priests, brothers, and sisters began to ask themselves if they were fulfilling their Christian vocation by teaching what others might teach as well or better, while the task of evangelization took a back seat.

Eventually, these concerns were expressed in actions. In one school in Nicaragua, for example, teaching literacy in poor neighborhoods became a requirement for graduation. In other cases Bible studies that incorporated justice concerns developed alongside the traditional "religion classes," which were obligatory and often ignored by the students. So an important network of youth groups was created under the tutelage of priests, brothers, and sisters who — despite the opposition they encountered from the more conservative members of their religious orders and from many parents of their students — became a true resource that nourished the grassroots movements.

Chapter 7

The Rise of a Prophetic Church

Enrique Dussel writes of the late 1960s:

> Together with developmentalism, a revolutionary current
> was running through Latin America. The Colombian guer-
> rilla priest Camilo Torres was killed in combat on February
> 15, 1966, and in 1967 Cuban revolutionary "Che" Gue-
> vara was killed in the mountains of Bolivia. In 1967
> Pope Paul VI released his encyclical *Populorum Progres-
> sio*, in which he spoke of "the international imperialism of
> money."...During this period the "theory of dependency"
> began to challenge "developmentalism," demonstrating the
> necessity not of *reforms*, but of a continent-wide structural
> *liberation*.
>   There was the Chinese Cultural Revolution of 1966,
> the Mexican student rebellion snuffed out in blood on
> October 2, 1968, in Tlatelolco, and, also in 1968, the
> Vietnam War demonstrations in Berkeley and the Paris
> "May."...Socialist Salvador Allende won the elections in
> Chile in 1970, and the pope released his encyclical *Octoges-
> ima Adveniens* (1971) in which he allowed for democratic
> socialism.[1]

In light of these events on the world scene, it is not surpris-
ing that beginning in the late 1960s, major changes occurred
in Central America, for example, the collapse of the Central
American Common Market and growing belligerence of student
and grassroots movements. In this atmosphere, the most progressive sectors of the Central American Catholic Church felt
the need to develop a ministry more in accord with the grassroots, as well as to deepen their understanding of their national

---

[1]Enrique Dussel, *Los últimos 50 años (1930–1985) en la historia de la Iglesia
en América Latina* (Bogotá: Indo-American Press Service, 1986), p. 36.

and regional situations, of the Medellín documents, and of the emerging theology of liberation.

Grassroots Ministry

As we have seen, within the Roman Catholic Church in Central America a significant current of opinion and practice already supported the struggle for justice. The Christian communities that were being formed, the youth groups, the Celebrations of the Word, the rural training centers, and other experiments were energized and confirmed by the Medellín Conference. We were at the beginning of a new period of greater conscientization[2] and biblical and theological development.

As Felix Jiménez notes in relation to St. Paul the Apostle parish of Managua:

> The message of Medellín has great importance for the parish; it confirmed what community members had been feeling about the changes that must occur in Latin America and in the church. For the first time in the history of church teaching, a religious document spoke of total liberation of the human being, and of change in economic, social, and political structures.[3]

From 1969 on, in practically every Central American country, church leaders and clergy gathered for study weeks on team ministry and seminars on theology and worship. The resulting process of renewal — in theology, ministry, and worship — ran deep. More and more sectors of the church — both those open to a liberation approach and those who advocated social reform — began to understand the mission of the church as *evangelization*, that is, as announcing God's saving will that calls for the human-ization and total liberation of human beings, a mission that must be exercised as service and never in an arrogant, authoritarian, or otherworldly manner.

---

[2]See above, p. 68.

[3]Félix Jiménez, "La parroquia de San Pablo Apóstol, germen de las CEBs in Nicaragua," in G. Girardi, B. Forcano, and J. M. Vigil, eds., *Nicaragua, trinchera teológica* (Salamanca, Spain: Lóguez; Managua: CAV, 1987), pp. 63–82.

This understanding of evangelization was in contradiction to the church's traditional alliance with the government and the ruling classes. Instead, it declared a preferential option for the poor.[4] It considered Jesus' announcement of the Reign of God as the core of the gospel and was committed to beginning to build God's Reign here on earth through struggle for a more just and communal society. Influenced by Medellín and confronted with a system of injustice and oppression that many had barely begun to calculate, an increasing number of pastoral workers began a process of conversion. This led to a growing identification with the suffering, humiliation, and frustrations of the poor, but also with their longings for liberation.

After Medellín, various lay ministries, the Christian base communities, and ministry among the indigenous people all blossomed. And commitment to the poorest and most persecuted continued to grow, although the response within the church was not always positive. In Nicaragua, an attempt to work with the bishops to plan new forms of ministry was met with fear, suspicion, envy, and arguments. In the end the bishops' conference suppressed the team that proposed the plan. Nonetheless, creative experimentation continued in many dioceses, although not in an organized way. In Costa Rica, the Medellín documents were practically ignored by the bishops. New initiatives here were isolated, which made it easy for the priests supporting them to be repressed. The renewal groups that arose in Costa Rica were mainly ecumenical, and acted apart from the official churches.

The new ministries were really of two types. One took place in the rural villages and urban slums through the approaches we already have mentioned (for example, Christian base communities, evangelization efforts that introduced biblical and liberation themes into traditional religious practices). Another was based in existing or newly developing institutions (for example, Catholic schools, training centers, radio schools).

---

[4]"The preferential option for the poor": A notion that became widespread throughout the Latin American churches after the Medellín conference. The option for the poor — both God's option and the church's — was understood as "preferential" but not exclusive, that is, the commitment was not meant to foster class hatred.

Church renewal led to much improved training of lay leaders, or catechists, who were now commonly called *Delegados de la Palabra* (Delegates of the Word). Except in Costa Rica, existing training centers were strengthened and new ones founded (for example, "Los Naranjos" in El Salvador, "Santa Clara" in Honduras).

As we already have seen, the growth of these new lay ministries in Central America was due especially to the serious shortage of priests. In any case, it resulted in an interesting experiment in lay leadership, principally in rural and indigenous communities. The new lay ministers respected the religious traditions and popular piety that were so deeply rooted in these communities. Indeed, these practices had long been sustained by those lay persons who had held religious responsibilities in areas lacking priestly attention (prayer leaders, guardians of the patron saint). This already existing religious leadership was taken very seriously when future Delegates of the Word were chosen, as well as when community activities were organized. In general, the emerging lay leadership was collective and democratic. Leaders were chosen not by the priests or sisters, but by the community; the leaders did not act alone, but in consultation with the community.

The educational approach and group dynamics techniques utilized in the training centers gave these natural leaders a greater awareness of their role as energizers of community life and as promoters of a deeper faith. So in the most progressive sectors of the Catholic Church in Central America a multitude of lay leaders arose with a new attitude that linked evangelization and total development of a community with its particular struggles.

In the smallest and most isolated villages, which a priest visited only a few times a year, Christians began to nourish their Christian and community life through Celebrations of the Word, which included songs, Bible reading (in native languages, in the case of the indigenous people), dialogue commentaries on the Bible readings, prayers and petitions, communion, and often a shared meal. Other ministries gradually developed within these communities, for example, readers, song leaders, teachers of children's catechism, teachers in pre-baptismal and pre-

marital preparation courses, and extraordinary ministers of the
Eucharist.[5]

Grassroots Communities and Political Movements

As the prophetic church movement gained headway among
the most open sectors of the Roman Catholic Church, grassroots political organizations were also growing, especially in the
countryside. The atmosphere where these new forms of ministry
were taking place had shifted. No longer was the situation only
one of injustice and exploitation. Signs of hope and resistance
were breaking out everywhere. And the ministries themselves
were signs of this change. But conflict generated by the changes
confronted the pastoral workers — lay and ordained — with
a difficult choice: to avoid the conflict by "spiritualizing" the
meaning of liberation, calling it inner or "personal" liberation,
or to give a religious meaning to this movement of liberation for
the oppressed. Many chose the second.

As elsewhere in Latin America, many Central American pastoral workers later joined political or military resistance organizations. This usually happened after years of ministry, when
all possibilities of change through democratic means had been
exhausted and the very people with whom they were working
had themselves decided to join the struggle.

Nonetheless, in Central America the pastoral workers made
an original contribution to the revolutionary movement.[6] They
brought their ministries into the liberation struggle, while maintaining their own clear Christian identity. That is, although they
were very aware of the dangerous political situation and the
struggle to change it, they continued to accompany the people
along their road to liberation precisely as Christian ministers.

In this "ministry of accompaniment" many people found a
spirituality that helped inspire their widespread decisions to join
the liberation struggles. They began to discover the links be-

---

[5]These were lay people authorized to distribute communion, that is, previously consecrated hosts, in the "extraordinary" circumstances in which no
priest was available to do so.

[6]See Pablo Richard, "La Iglesia que nace en América Central," in Cayetano
de Lella, ed., *Cristianismo y liberación en América Central* (Mexico City: Ediciones Nuevomar, 1984), pp. 31–32.

tween their Christian belief in God's Reign and the urgent need for radical change in their communities and countries.

Perhaps the most crucial impact of the church's new directions was the breaking down a fatalistic worldview among the Central American people, especially the peasants. In a fatalistic worldview, "whatever is, is God's will"; that is, the established political and social order is seen as the very order of nature, and therefore is as God desires. Although it is going too far to say, as some authors do, that this new religious understanding, this increased awareness, or "conscientization," was the "engine" that propelled the Central American revolutionary movement of the 1970s, it is certainly true that it would have been much more difficult for the rural people to have joined the movement in such large numbers had this fatalistic worldview not first been challenged.

Central to church renewal were the Christian base communities.[7] These developed on plantations and estates, in villages and in city slums. As we have seen, they were small groups of Christians who met to converse, meditate, pray, and celebrate their faith, always in light of their actual circumstances, and who tried to apply the conclusions of their community reflection to their daily lives.

In the regular meetings of the Christian base communities, Bible reading and reflection had a central place. For so long a "closed book" for the Central American poor, the Bible now revealed to them the Word of God in all its originality. In this way, the Christians in the communities began to discover the roots of their problems and their suffering. They began to understand the message of salvation as a liberation that begins here and now in this world, and to see that message of liberation had very much to do with the oppression and exploitation they experienced. Consequently, the groups' understanding of their actual situation was woven together with their understanding of the biblical message: the people became the interpreters of Scripture.[8]

---

[7]See above, p. 8.

[8]See Ernesto Cardenal, *The Gospel in Solentiname*, 4 vols. (Maryknoll, NY: Orbis Books, 1976–82); see also Robert McAfee Brown, *Unexpected News: Reading the Bible with Third World Eyes* (Philadelphia: Westminster, 1984).

READING THE BIBLE IN A BASE COMMUNITY

Solentiname is a group of islands in Lake Nicaragua. There Nicaraguan priest Ernesto Cardenal established a small Christian community among the campesinos. Each Sunday they together commented on the Gospels. The following transcriptions of their conversation were made during the time Somoza was in power. After the revolution in 1979, Cardenal, who is also a poet, became Minister of Culture in the Sandinista government.

The Rich Epicure and Poor Lazarus
Luke 16:19–31

It's the parable of the rich man who had parties every day, while the poor man was at his door covered with sores.

FELIPE: "I think the poor man here stands for all the poor, and the rich man for all the rich. The poor man is saved and the rich man is damned. That's the story, a very simple one, that Jesus tells us."

GLORIA: "The rich man's sin was that he had no compassion. Poverty was at his door, and that didn't disturb him at his parties."

WILLIAM: "The traditional interpretation of this passage is wrong and is used for exploitation. The poor have been led to believe that they must patiently endure because after death they're going to be better off and that the rich will get their punishment."

FELIPE: "As I see it, this passage was to threaten the rich so they wouldn't go on exploiting. But it seems it turned out the opposite: it's used to pacify the people."

OLIVIA: "I think the word of God has been very badly preached, and the church is much to blame for this. It's because the Gospel hasn't been well preached that we have a society still divided between rich and poor. There are few places like Solentiname where the Gospel is preached and we understand it. Also, it's we poor people who understand it. Unfortunately, the rich don't come to hear it. Where the rich are, there's no preaching like that."

MARIITA: "The rich man's sin was not sharing — not sharing with everybody, that is, with the poor too; because he *did* share with the rich: the Gospel says he gave parties every day."

JULIO: "They wouldn't invite the poor; they'd get their houses dirty."

ERNESTO: "I believe this parable was not to console the poor but rather to threaten the rich; but as you said, William, it has had the opposite effect, because the rich wouldn't heed it. But Christ himself is saying that in this parable: that the rich pay no attention to the Bible."

OSCAR: "It seems like it doesn't do any good to be reading the Bible, then, because if you don't want to change the social order, you might as well be reading any damned thing, you might as well be reading any stupid book."

ERNESTO: "It seems to me that Jesus' principal message is that the rich aren't going to be convinced even with the Bible, not even with a dead man coming to life — and not even with Jesus' resurrection."

The Beatitudes
Matt. 5:1–12

OLIVIA: "The poor in spirit or the poor in God are the poor, but provided they have the spirit of the oppressed and not of the oppressor, provided they don't have the mentality of the rich."

Old TOMAS: "Because we poor people can also have pride, like the rich."

ALEJANDRO: "What we see here is that there are two things. One is the reign of God, which is the reign of love, of equality, where we must all be like brothers and sisters; and the other thing is the system we have, which isn't brand new, it's centuries old, the system of rich and poor, where business is business."

ANGEL: "That's why it seems to me that we have to interpret carefully. If we just stick to the fact that we're poor and God has said that the reign of God is for the poor, then we'd end up saying that, well, because we're poor we already have the reign of God and we can do anything."

ERNESTO: "I've just had a visit from a young fellow from the north, from Estelí, from a poor town. He is a *campesino* — like yourselves — and he was saying that there to get together for their Masses, first they have to ask permission from the police, and the police captain said that those gatherings were dangerous. The captain is right, for they gather there to talk about the Gospels...."

Another typically Central American phenomenon was the way Christian base communities, as entire communities maintaining their Christian identity, entered into the grassroots political movements. So it was not simply individual Christians who joined the liberation struggles, but complete and organized communities. This greatly extended the influence of the pastoral workers. The Christian base communities became centers of liberating evangelization and teachers of faith. Grassroots Christianity became a unique spiritual force in mobilizing the people for their total liberation.

This explains why grassroots organizations frequently found in the religious organizations — the Christian base communities and other grassroots church groups, both Protestant and Catholic, as well as other traditional groups like the old confraternities — the point of contact with the peasant and urban slum communities. Moreover, religious organizations were often the only organizations in these communities.

This process of conscientization and religious organization heightened the "crisis of credibility" in the existing social and political arrangements. The governments and ruling classes of these countries, though they still could count on many bishops and priests to more or less unconditionally support their actions, became increasingly concerned that they could no longer depend on even conditional support from broad sectors of the church.

> With religious legitimation lost, and the myth of a so-called natural order broken, there was no way to gain credibility in the eyes of the people other than through social change; the alternative was a show of power through a policy of massive repression. Although every government made timid efforts at social reform, such changes were unacceptable to the intransigent ruling classes; thus, their only viable option for retaining power was to resort to violent repression.[9]

---

[9]Ignacio Martín Baró, *Iglesia y revolución en El Salvador* (San Salvador: mimeo, 1985), pp. 9–10

Persecuted Communities

Progressive priests and sisters who shared the developmentalist mentality — with the best of intentions, but without adequate tools of analysis — generally took a long time to realize that their approach to society and ministry meshed very well with the political and economic programs of the U.S. business community and its local colleagues.

But as many in the church became more and more aware of their people's real situation, the division between the church of Christendom model and the new prophetic church model became ever clearer. One sign of this break was that an increasing number of priests and sisters left their wealthy parishes, elite lay movements, and private schools for upper-class children to move to the city slums or poor rural areas.

These pastoral workers swelled the ranks of those who had long been working among the poor in those areas. Their experience transformed their understanding of the real forces that cause poverty and block programs for the advancement and economic independence of the rural and urban poor.

The local powers — landowners and business people who had close links to the army and the police — immediately felt threatened by the attempts of the poor to achieve economic independence. Their response included attacks on cooperatives, acts of sabotage (for example, burning crops, destroying trucks), payoffs for collaborators, and murder of grassroots leaders. Such acts quickly educated the pastoral workers in the nature of the region's social conflicts. In turn their commitment to the exploited and oppressed people intensified. In many cases, pastoral workers began to accept political responsibilities and to join in actions of community self-defense and even armed struggle.

This profound transformation of religious practice and theological understanding was taking place amid an acute social crisis in the Central American societies. Radical protests by various oppressed groups increased markedly, protest that helped explain the increased political awareness and religious radicalization.

The growing participation of militant Christians, pastoral agents, and Christian base communities in the grassroots movements caused the initial suspicions of many landowners, business people, and military officers to turn quickly into open hostility. At various estates and factories, the most active Christian leaders began to be fired for "meddling in nonsense." Soon great waves of violent repression were unleashed.

In 1975 this new stage of conflict erupted in blood in El Salvador and Honduras (the massacres at "La Cayetana" and "Tres Calles," and the "Crime of Olancho"). By 1977, a real persecution of the churches was evident. This persecution, rigorously following the lines of the so-called Banzer Plan,[10] included acts of violence against persons and institutions, as well as furious smear campaigns in the media.

The conflicts between the institutional church and the Central American ruling classes was no longer only a power struggle at the level of church-state relations. Now it became fiercer and more local, with conflicts between the Christian base communities, the parishes, and the rural training centers on the one hand, and the local powers on the other.

The persecution was discussed within the Christian base communities, with many prayers for strength. The actions and the fate of Moses, the prophets, and Jesus of Nazareth came to be understood with a clarity previously unknown: their anguish and suffering in their commitment and the consequences of their dedication; the desire to flee, to keep silent; and the burning within that drove them on without faltering. And so there was born a new generation of martyrs, of witnesses to the faith.

But perhaps more important than the actions of Christians in the grassroots movements has been the spirit that the prophetic church has communicated to Central American struggles for liberation. The poor of the region — those for whom religion is still a basic frame of reference — have found strength to undergo the terrible hardships of war without losing their generosity and hope despite the prolonged struggle. Central American Christians do not seek to sacrifice their own lives as a burnt offering on the altar of some absolute cause, but they do

---

[10]The "Banzer Plan," formulated in 1975 under the Bolivian government of Hugo Banzer, listed tactics for discrediting progressive church leaders and dividing the church, including planting subversive documents on church premises.

find in faith a key for interpreting the meaning of the struggle for freedom and justice.

Of course, the process of conscientization we have described and its consequent revolutionary commitment do not apply to all Christians of the region, nor to the entire Roman Catholic Church. In fact, the new prophetic church model was born in harsh conflict with many of the bishops, as well as with elitist or otherworldly lay movements, promoted by pastoral workers aligned with business interests.

A Church Divided

We will not understand this conflict unless we understand two important pieces of recent Central American history. First, the local ruling classes survived the economic crisis of the 1930s by taking a hard political line — which brought forth the cruel and violent dictatorships already described.[11] These dictatorships, in large measure, maintained their control by the direct and constant support of the U.S. government. Second, industrialization, as we saw in Chapter 3, occurred only recently, in the 1960s, during a period of increased foreign investment.

The combination and timing of these two developments prevented any significant growth of a populist or democratic middle class. Nor did democratic governments have a chance to develop in the Central American countries. Experiments in populism or democratic participation rested on a very weak base, and they were either stopped before they got started (as in Guatemala), or were short-lived (as in Honduras and El Salvador). Only in Costa Rica could some democratic processes get underway. So Central America underwent its own unique development, in which the confrontation between the people and the ruling classes was extremely direct and violent.

Nor could the Central American church reap the benefits of the kind of "reformist synthesis" between faith and politics that had occurred elsewhere in Latin America. In other countries, the influence of a larger, more educated middle class enabled bishops to become more flexible and open to the rise of the new prophetic church model. But in Central America the new model

---

[11]See above, pp. 40–47.

developed more rapidly and directly out of the grassroots movement; thus it has deeper roots among the poor than in other
parts of Latin America. For the same reason the confrontation
between the prophetic church and the church of Christendom
has been sharper.

In some instances, when extreme repressive actions directly
touch the church institution itself, the majority of the bishops
and other sectors of the church stand with the prophetic church
and confront the governments and repressive forces linked to
the military or police. But the conflict between the two models
continues.

So the new church model arising from Vatican II and Medellín, while it unifies and energizes, has also produced deep
divisions in the church.

> This is a much more radical division than the old divisions
> between the hierarchy and the faithful, or between differ-
> ent schools of theology, for it is God who is responsible
> for the division; the reason for the division is the gospel of
> Jesus and the poor of this world. The challenges issued to
> the church by the poor of this world and, through them,
> by God are these: "What have you done to your broth-
> ers and sisters?" "What have you done for the injured on
> the side of the road?" These are ultimate questions, un-
> avoidable, which cannot be silenced or smoothed over by
> church maneuvering. Since everyone does not respond to
> these challenges in the same way, and since it is difficult
> to respond in a Christian way, grave divisions arise within
> the church.[12]

With the appearance of a prophetic church, committed to the
poor, oppressed, and exploited people of Central America, the
tension within the church is now established between the reformist sectors — supported by the traditionalists — who are
attempting to preserve the Christendom model, and the sectors
committed to liberation, who advocate a prophetic church.

---

[12]"Hacia dónde va la Iglesia," in ECA 434 (December 1984), p. 876.

Chapter 8

The Present Regional Crisis

Central America is going through the greatest crisis in its entire history — an economic, political, and, above all, social crisis deeper and more widespread than that of the 1930s. These countries find themselves more and more polarized — not only between classes, but between broader coalitions. On one side is the people's coalition, made up of peasants, workers, and other poor people, but also intellectuals and progressive sectors in the churches. On the other side is a kind of anti-people's coalition, which includes the traditional ruling classes, the business class, and a good portion of the conservative Roman Catholic bishops and other conservative sectors of the churches.

It is a political crisis, because social revolution in Central America presupposes an attack on the entire political system. To use Xabier Gorostiaga's words, this revolution gives rise to a "logic of the masses" opposed to the old "logic of capitalism."[1] This new logic unites intellectuals, church people, and even some business people, who do not find any alternatives coming from either the foreign centers of international power nor from the local ruling classes. According to Gorostiaga, it is no longer possible to make compromises to reform the system, given U.S. policy toward the region, which has allowed the political center to collapse. The recent electoral defeat of the Christian Democrats by the right wing in El Salvador is a very clear example of this. The full dimensions of the regional crisis were demonstrated in the early 1980s.

The "Reagan Plan" for the Region

Gorostiaga believes that the present crisis is actually a crisis of control because there is today no center of world power, as there was, for example, when England and the United States were

---

[1] Xabier Gorostiaga, "Horizonte geopolítico y teología de la liberación," in *Solidaridad* (Colombia), June 1988, pp. 26–37.

pitted against the German threat. At stake in the current crisis is control of world power.

After the acute crisis of political power with Vietnam, Watergate, and the weak administrations of Lyndon Johnson, Gerald Ford, and Jimmy Carter, the United States under Ronald Reagan tried to regain world leadership. The "Reagan Plan" was part of the conservative response (a continuous thread in United States political history), which saw itself as defending the basic principles on which the nation was founded.

This program based U.S. foreign policy on "containing" the Soviet threat. From this point of view the primary conflict on the global level is confrontation between East and West. In the Reagan era, policy toward the Soviet Union was reformulated to eliminate the military "gap" between the two countries. It was believed that this hard-line policy toward the Soviets would strengthen the alliance with Western Europe and Japan and would restore to the U.S. leadership within the Western world.

In Latin America and the Caribbean, the U.S. policy involved, on the one hand, an improvement of relations with "friendly" countries, some of which had been affected by the human rights policy of the Carter administration (such as Chile, Argentina, Guatemala). On the other hand, harsh actions were taken against regimes seen as "hostile" to U.S. interests (such as Cuba, Grenada, and Nicaragua).

These foreign policy objectives were promoted in various ways. First, the military budget was substantially increased and the intelligence-gathering apparatus was strengthened. Economic and military aid was employed to spread support for "the American way of life." Finally the model of the free market was promoted as the best way to encourage democracy and economic growth.

In the case of Central America (with the exception of Nicaragua) the attempt to impose a new model of control pushed Central American societies toward reorganizing themselves in the service of great international corporations along with their local allies (who were, naturally, opposed to the interests of the poor). Indeed, according to the astute observation of Abelardo Morales, the possibilities for action in these small nations:

are not totally controlled by external factors, as those who attribute the crisis exclusively to external factors would explain it.... The actual decisions pass through a domestic process in which decision makers on the national level act in accord with their own assessments and objectives — which are often shaped by outside powers.[2]

In this new model of control, the most relevant features are:

Economic: The model is against government intervention and reforms. The market is extolled as the path to the absolute good of humanity; it is the panacea for all of society's problems.

In the free market economy:

• The national economies revert to private control, with a dismantling of the welfare state and government-controlled businesses.

• Foreign companies are given open and preferential admittance to the region.

• Industrialization is no longer a priority, with a resulting crisis for small and middle-sized industries.

• Industrial, commercial, and financial free trade zones are established for the benefit of foreign corporations.

• Financial institutions, as well as international aid agencies (the International Monetary Fund, the World Bank, the U.S. Agency for International Development) and international banks impose economic policies that generate greater inflation, lower salaries, and higher unemployment.

• The pressure of foreign debt subjects the governments of the region to a new and dangerous dependency, which creates even greater poverty and oppression.

Political: The national security apparatus, that is, the military and police, is strengthened, but now different ways of showing that a government is legitimate are emphasized. The two primary new mechanisms of legitimation are elections and the political proposals of reformist parties.

Elections were held in Guatemala, El Salvador, and Honduras, but without any significant political or social changes to

---

[2]Abelardo Morales, *Costa Rica: el ajuste estructural y el dilema de la integración regional* (San José, Costa Rica: CEDECO, 1989), pp. 7–8.

assure authentic democratic participation. The reformist political proposals, primarily those of the Social Christian and Christian Democratic parties, have been utilized with the same end, namely, to cover up and legitimate the repression of the poor.

Ideological: Total control of the media (the press, radio, and television) is in the hands of the local power structure, allied with foreign investors, above all from the United States. Cultural domination is intensified, and a foreign, consumer-oriented, and violent culture is imposed upon the Central American people.

Religious: As a part of the ideological, theological, and political offensive against the progressive churches and theologies of liberation in Latin America (and in the United States as well), there is an invasion of new religious movements, including the so-called electronic church. These tend to emphasize individual religious experience. Campaigns are launched to intimidate the churches and confine them also to the concerns of private and otherworldly spirituality. To accomplish this, the media, politicians, businesses, and the military constantly cry "communism" against any prophetic activity of the churches in society.

Thus the Sandinista movement in Nicaragua and the liberation movements in other Central American countries have had to confront a powerful administration with the clearest plan for control of the region that the United States has had since World War II. But the attempt of the United States to regain control of the West faced direct conflict in its own "backyard" that affected its image in the world. Although the Reagan Plan viewed Central America as an opportunity to regain global control, the plan did not succeed. Neither Western Europe nor Canada agreed with the Reagan administration's policy toward the region. Even U.S. public opinion, especially that of the churches, opposed the policy.

The demands for independence and self-determination of the Central American people are a clear example of what many have called a North-South conflict, that is, between the industrialized nations of the northern part of the globe and the poor nations of the South. But the Reagan administration did not admit that these demands were legitimate. It kept trying to make the problem of these poor nations to its south into an East-West ("communism" versus "free world") conflict. This was the only way it could justify its policy of militarization and the threat of force in Central America.

But if we analyze, for example, the economic changes that the Sandinistas have brought about in Nicaragua, we see that with the exception of the nationalization of foreign trade they are fundamentally the same as those suggested by the Alliance for Progress. The real issue is not so much specific changes or how radical they are, but who controls the change. And the old ruling classes, the middle class, and the business leaders are no longer in charge. A new protagonist has emerged: the people's coalitions. This is what neither the U.S. nor the local ruling classes can tolerate: that the people should be in control.

Myths of Development

What in Central America we call the "logic of the majority" is creating a new understanding of development that breaks with the great economic myths. One such myth the "trickle-down theory," which says that when there is economic growth a kind of "invisible hand" distributes wealth so that it finally reaches the poor. Central America is the best example that this theory is not true; on the contrary, wealth has been concentrated in fewer hands.

In fact, between 1950 and 1978 the region registered the most rapid economic growth in the world. Yes, Central America had sustained economic growth at an annual rate of 6 percent for twenty-eight years. Only Singapore, Hong Kong, South Korea, and Taiwan had similar growth. Nevertheless, as we have already seen in Chapter 3, despite the great changes that occurred in those three decades of growth, the benefits went to a small minority, and the poverty of the great majority of people increased. Thus the CEPAL[3] poll of 1980 showed that two-thirds of Central Americans lived below poverty levels and almost half in severe poverty. The great truths about our region, which cannot be hidden or justified and which horrify our Christian conscience, are the wretched conditions of the Central American people and the repression that crushes them. Because of this, after three

---

[3]See above, p. 33.

decades of economic growth, the region exploded in three violent eruptions: in Nicaragua, in El Salvador, and in Guatemala. As Gorostiaga says:

> At times we forget that the largest massacres and the greatest number of deaths occurred in Guatemala. Somoza was an "angel" compared with the killing sprees of the Guatemalan army against the indigenous people and peasants.[4]

Between 1980 and 1988 all the countries of the region had negative per capita economic growth. It is estimated that in El Salvador, for example, the per capita consumption in 1988 was less than that of 1963, while in Guatemala it was at 1971 levels. Even in Nicaragua, military recruitment, the lack of production in combat zones, and rampant inflation (which encourages speculative activities more than productive ones), have all had a negative effect on the distribution of income.

Of course the consequences of the decline in growth rates are varied. To the overall lower standard of living we must add unemployment. Thus, for example, from 1980 to 1988 unemployment rose in Guatemala from 2.2 percent to 14.5 percent; in Honduras, from 15.2 percent to 30 percent; and in El Salvador, from 16 percent to 33 percent. And these figures do not show the increase in underemployment and in the numbers of those who must hold down more than one job.

The other great regional problem is foreign debt. The Central American countries find themselves caught in a vicious circle of financial asphyxiation, with a growing inability to get on top of the situation. Not all the countries are affected in the same way. At the end of 1986, the sum of Central American debt was 17.2 billion dollars, of which 5.7 billion was owed by Nicaragua, 3.74 billion by Costa Rica, 2.92 billion by Honduras, 2.64 billion by Guatemala, and 2.1 billion by El Salvador. An indication of the burden that interest on the debt represents for those countries is that, in 1978, 11 percent of the value of exports was

---

[4]Xabier Gorostiaga, "Perspectivas sociopolíticas y teológicas sobre la paz en Centroamérica," in *Amanecer* (Nicaragua), January–February 1989, p. 33.

required to service the debt, but in 1987 this percentage had increased to more than 40 percent (48 percent in the case of El Salvador).

On the other hand, El Salvador, Honduras, and Costa Rica are the countries that, after Israel, received the greatest amount of U.S. assistance in per capita terms during the 1980s. In spite of this aid, their economies have descended to 1970 levels. (Nicaragua's economy also declined, but Nicaragua has endured a war of aggression and been subjected to a commercial embargo and financial boycott by the U.S. government.) This situation has also debunked another great myth of economic theory: that foreign aid produces development. Gorostiaga tells us:

We now know more about development. We know better that development does not only depend on growth, nor just on foreign aid, on international capitalism, on capital flow.... All this can help, but this is not development.[5]

Gorostiaga also insists that the great problem of Central America is not poverty, but injustice, which in turn produces war. And poverty can indeed be eradicated from the region, especially because Central America is so strategically important for international commerce between the Pacific and the Atlantic. But, says Gorostiaga,

Central America has always been used: by the Spanish conquistadors to "discover" the Pacific; by the pirates in colonial times to capture the gold of the galleons; by the gold diggers during the gold rush in California, who crossed Nicaragua or Panama to transport their gold; by the expansion of world commerce through the Panama Canal. Now Central America has become one of the principal links in international drug traffic. The whole world uses us and does not allow Central America to create its own solution. It is for this that we are fighting.[6]

---

[5]Xabier Gorostiaga, "Horizonte geopolítico y teología de la liberación," in *Solidaridad* (Colombia), June 1988, p. 31.

[6]Ibid.

Low Intensity Warfare

Undoubtedly the most outstanding feature of the present Central American situation is the prolongation and expansion of armed conflict throughout the entire region. Central America is at war: open and declared war in El Salvador, and at least until recently in Nicaragua; incipient war, more or less hidden, in Guatemala. It is war that in one way or another affects all the countries of Central America.

The U.S. military strategy has been called "low intensity warfare." For those who are suffering the consequences, however, it does not appear to be a war of "low intensity." This strategy is to discredit and isolate the guerrillas, undermining their political support. It has included U.S. military aid for counterinsurgency operations carried on by Central American governments or, in the case of Nicaragua, support for the counterrevolutionary Contras. Operations have included rescue missions, aid in situations of conflict, covert actions, and plans for military, political, and economic destabilization.

The main objective of low intensity warfare is to separate the people from the guerrilla movement, and this is sometimes accomplished simply by relocating entire groups of people — thus creating thousands of refugees. Furthermore, since the principal strategy is to wage a war of exhaustion, the goal is to prolong conflict so that the region is permanently under military control, with the resulting social and political costs.

Of course, low intensity warfare is very much at odds with a policy of economic recovery, which is basic to any program to diminish social unrest. The economic programs related to low intensity warfare (such as civic action, humanitarian aid, propaganda operations, and plans for local development) only seek to disguise the repression practiced by the military governments and security forces, but these programs in no way deal with the real economic problems.

In the 1980s, the regime in Guatemala used a threefold strategy to counteract grassroots protest and resistance in the rural areas: massacres, the establishment of civilian patrols to enforce its policies, and the forced movement of entire populations into "model villages." As a result more than a hundred thousand

Guatemalan refugees are living in Mexico, and more than a million people are displaced within the country itself. Moreover, the uprooting of indigenous communities contributes to the destruction of their cultural base and their social identity.

In El Salvador, the number of displaced people within the country itself has reached about 600,000. In 1988 the Salvadoran unemployment rate was more than 30 percent, while it was estimated that one-fifth of the national income came from money sent by Salvadorans living outside the country, principally in the United States.

The combination of militarization and of massive U.S. "aid" has brought the Central American countries to a situation of great dependency on the USA. During the 1980s in Honduras the virtual occupation of much territory by U.S. troops and the Nicaraguan counterrevolutionaries as well as the construction of huge military installations turned the country into an enormous base from which to fight the Sandinistas in Nicaragua. In 1987 alone El Salvador received 608 million dollars in "official" aid, more than the national budget for that year. In fact all the countries in the region are very dependent on foreign aid and loans.

The huge costs of this increased militarization mean even less money is available to develop the economies in ways that could relieve poverty. In Nicaragua more than 50 percent of the national budget goes to defense. In El Salvador about 50 percent of the national budget is consumed by the costs of the internal war; in Guatemala it is 29 percent. Another result of war in the region is that large numbers of young people are required as military personnel.

Between 1981 and 1988 more than 100,000 people were killed in the fighting, and the numbers of those left as widows and orphans and those injured, mutilated, and displaced would be in the millions if they could be counted.

In addition to all their suffering and the suffering of their families, we must also bear in mind the economic destruction caused by war, which already reaches many millions of dollars. And the military maneuvers, the bombings, and the other effects of war have accelerated the destruction of the region's natural resources.

This prolongation of armed conflict, a strategy that we were well aware of by 1983, has extremely serious consequences in each Central American country. Furthermore, it is clear that the policy of the Reagan administration reached a "dead-end." Indeed, with this concise phrase former secretary of state George Shultz summed up the failure of a policy that, through low intensity warfare, tried quickly both to resolve the Salvadoran situation and to root out the "Sandinista cancer." The bankruptcy of this policy is seen at various levels.

On the Military Level. In Nicaragua, the Contras' organization has been severely wounded; bold initiatives at negotiation divided it, immobilized it, and obliged it to retreat to Honduras. In El Salvador, despite the advances made by the U.S.-Salvadoran counterinsurgency strategy, the FMLN[7] has gained strength politically and militarily, taking the initiative both in the war and in political proposals to end the war with reasonable negotiations. Grassroots movements have been revitalized at every level. The means chosen by the Reagan administration to administer the entire plan, the centrist Christian Democratic government of José Napoleón Duarte, virtually collapsed because of its inability to control the country's economy, rampant corruption, attacks by the FMLN, rapidly expanding grassroots resistance, and the intransigence of the business people and landowners.

In Guatemala the guerrilla movement at first remained small, but later it was able to take advantage of the breathing room provided by the "opening for democracy." But the Christian Democratic government of Vinicio Cerezo has been caught between grassroots demands and the inflexibility of the military, business, and ruling classes. Nonetheless, the Reagan administration was unable to convince Cerezo to participate in the diplomatic isolation of the Sandinista government of Nicaragua. In 1988 the antiguerrilla military offensive fell apart, and this failure has practically ruined the government of Cerezo and the plan of modernization with democracy, which was supported by some groups in the armed forces. The armed forces' role became even

---

[7]The Farabundo Martí National Liberation Front, a coalition of Salvadoran guerrilla organizations named after the leader of the aborted 1932 uprising.

clearer in some recent attempts by military groups to overthrow the government. Furthermore the URNG (Guatemalan National Revolutionary Union, the guerrilla movement) has grown in military strength and spread through more of the country, making proposals to negotiate with the government.

In Honduras a resistance movement within the army has gained strength — weary of the way the Honduran military allows the presence of Contra camps in Honduran territory. Moreover, there have been recent outbreaks of guerrilla resistance and spontaneous demonstrations protesting the U.S. embassy's meddling in the internal affairs of Honduras.

On the Economic Level. As already mentioned, the prolonged political-military conflict has sharpened the economic crisis. So the Reagan administration was obliged to continue economic subsidies to El Salvador, Honduras, and Costa Rica. The economic crisis that has afflicted Guatemala since 1985 probably means that this country will also soon become a kind of "economic protectorate" of the U.S.

Local business groups and ruling classes have taken advantage of U.S. subsidies in order to withdraw their own investments from the national economies. At the same time they have stubbornly refused to assume any financial responsibility for the "war taxes"; that is, they have refused to pay any part of the price of their own defense against the grassroots resistance and to help defray the deficits of their own governments.

The widespread administrative corruption of the governments and the growing costs of maintaining the economic protectorates (which saps the economic strength of the U.S.), diminish any hopes that the Bush administration may have of continuing to subsidize these economies on a large scale.

On the Political Level. The "democratization" promoted during recent years by U.S. foreign policy — that is, "limited democracies" in accord with the plan for the region — quickly collapsed because it could not satisfy the people's demands for profound social and democratic reforms.

This process represented a kind of "democratic toll" paid by the business sector, the ruling class, and the military to stay in power. But the process seems only to have discredited the centrist position (the kind of government represented by Duarte in El Salvador) and has left the U.S. without clear political options in the face of a prolonged conflict. The growing political instability of the Central American countries is alarming.

In El Salvador the victory of the right-wing ARENA party (National Republican Alliance) in the parliamentary and mayoral elections in 1988 began the collapse of the centrist party's efforts to implement a counterinsurgency plan. The rise to power of hard-line officers in the armed forces, the intensification of death-squad violence, the new show of military power of the FMLN,[8] increased grassroots resistance, and the victory of ARENA in the presidential elections reveal just how great the instability is. It appears that President Bush will have no other recourse than to cooperate with the right-wing government, which claims the right to design the counterinsurgency strategy and manage the war.

In Guatemala the failure of the military offensive against the guerrillas in 1988 and the agreement between the government and UASP (Union of Labor and Popular Action, which represents many grassroots groups) angered an important faction of military officers and the business sector. The discontent led to the attempted coup of May 1988 (repeated just one year later), and has left the government of Vinicio Cerezo very weak. The result has been political crackdowns, the purchase of new armaments from the U.S., an increase in U.S. military aid to the armed forces, and the refusal to allow the URNG[9] to participate in any way in national dialogue.

On the Cultural Level. The Central American people have become more and more deeply divided over two choices: between self-determination and social transformation on the one hand, or submission to the U.S. and maintenance of the status quo on the other. This split within each country into two cultures prevents a stable and lasting solution to the crisis the U.S. faces in the region. U.S. foreign policy, rather than guaranteeing a new cultural consensus, has provoked further polarization.

On the International Level. Within the last decade the U.S. government's involvement has become more and more intense

---

[8]See note above, p. 94.
[9]See above, p. 95.

and direct (it has included, for example, the mining of ports, military maneuvers, military advisors, sophisticated military equipment, financing the Nicaraguan counterrevolutionaries). These actions have provoked growing differences with many U.S. allies, both Latin American and European.

Perspectives on Development and Peace

There is a growing consensus that the present Central American crisis is not simply a fleeting phenomenon:

> Nor does it represent a temporary downturn in the development of these dependent societies. Nor will a solution be reached by a simple internal adjustment of national structures.... The solution to the crisis cannot be a return to the society that existed before 1979; on the contrary, the region must undergo a profound transformation.[10]

It is not so easy to come to a consensus about the solution to the crisis, because Central America's diverse political forces variously support or attack economic and political proposals for change. Abelardo Morales believes that at present there are three options for regional development. The first, which he calls *supply-side openness*, corresponds to the model already described that the Reagan administration sought to impose. This option

> considers that the production of nontraditional, exportable goods represents the best possibility for economic growth. It suggests that these countries develop their comparative advantages (through the offer of cheap manual labor) and compete for foreign markets.[11]

Although this option has been promoted in every Central American country except Nicaragua, it has been most successful in Costa Rica. Its results have been more modest in Honduras, El Salvador, and Guatemala.

---

[10]Abelardo Morales, *Costa Rica: el ajuste estructural y el dilema de la integración regional* (San José, Costa Rica: CEDECO, 1989), p. 9.

[11]Ibid., p. 10.

The second option, called *mixed* by Morales, proposes to strengthen the structures created in the 1970s under the Central American Common Market to adapt the industrial plants to the needs of the international market. This focus is promoted by the industrial business sector, which believes that the Central American market alone is not large enough to produce or consume all its own goods.

The third option, called *integrational*, aims to achieve less foreign dependency and greater independence for the countries in the area by integrating Central American economies with the economies of the other Latin American countries. From this point of view, the principal goal of economic growth and development is to meet the basic needs of the region's own people. This approach would establish mechanisms to distribute income more justly and to involve the majority of the people in the various levels of development. The Nicaraguan government has put such a plan into place, although U.S. aggression has seriously undermined the success of its experiments.

The first two models look to the "economic miracles" accomplished in the countries of the Pacific Rim (South Korea, Taiwan, Hong King, Singapore), apparently without realizing that the conditions that make their economic growth possible would be almost impossible to duplicate in Central America.

Xabier Gorostiaga, who has worked in recent years on two U.S. commissions on Central America — the Inter-American Dialogue and the International Commission for Central American Recovery and Development (the Sanford Commission[12]) — believes that the present moment is ideal to move toward a negotiated solution to the Central American conflict. His suggestion is made in the context of a worldwide easing of political tension, which includes getting beyond the "satanization" of adversaries (as between the U.S. and the U.S.S.R.); the opening of Eastern Europe; demilitarization around the world; and negotiated solutions to various regional conflicts (for example, Afghanistan, Angola, Cambodia).

---

[12]A nongovernmental commission assembled by U.S. Senator Terry Sanford, with members from twenty nations. Central Americans co-chair the commission and each of its five committees.

Moreover, this is a moment of great strategic importance for Central America. Western Europe will become a united economy beginning in 1992, and it has begun to exercise an independent foreign policy toward Latin America, with a special aid plan for Central America. Likewise, Japan has shown a special interest that Central America, the bridge between the Pacific and the Atlantic, achieve a stability that will allow it to become a base of operations for Japanese commerce and exports to Latin America.

There has also been a change in Washington. At this writing it appears that Central American policy will be more pragmatic. It is likely that the low intensity conflict strategy will be modified to lessen the military role but maintain political, economic, and diplomatic pressure, using more sophisticated forms of control and coercion. The great danger is that this policy might distract international attention from Central America by creating the impression that an era of peace, democracy, and development has arrived. But the goal of real peace, democracy, and development cannot be achieved as long as the causes of crisis and conflict continue, that is, while poverty, injustice, and political disenfranchisement are not overcome and the majority of the people are excluded from the decisions that shape their lives.

The short-term challenge will be to negotiate an end to the conflict with stable and just conditions for all those involved. This, in turn, would allow for a truly innovative democratic dynamism in which grassroots programs and regional and national goals would all have a real part. The alternative is the "dead-end street" of tragic and exhausting war.

Chapter 9

The Present Church Conflict

As we saw in the last chapter, profound changes took place in Central America during the 1980s. A principal aspect of the new situation was that the United States presence in the region was shaped by neoconservative policy. Not only did this presence mean increased militarization; this neoconservative strategy also focused on a war of ideas. In this ideological struggle, religion and the forms religion takes in the society are considered very important.

Neoconservatism manipulates the media very successfully. The progressive sectors of the church, on the other hand, have not had a media strategy of their own, and so have been unable to reach the majority of the people.

Retrenchment

The Latin American Roman Catholic Church in general and the Central American church in particular are today far removed from the times of high excitement that followed Vatican Council II and the Latin American bishops' conference at Medellín. The church is passing through a "winter season," as German theologian Karl Rahner said, or through a retrenchment, as others would have it.

Some who study the church see this retrenchment as damaging and unnecessary. They believe that the Vatican Council can still inspire the church and that its spirit has still not been fully accepted. Likewise, they believe that putting the conclusions of the Medellín Conference into practice allowed the Latin American church to change and grow as a prophetic church. And while they recognize that this new model of church has limitations and has made mistakes, they are convinced that its impact has been very positive.

They point out that the Latin American church has found its true place among the poor and that church unity and ecumenism among the various denominations has increased, all amid great creativity in theology, worship, and ministry. This church has defended the lives and the rights of the poor, has accompanied them in their struggles for liberation, and has suffered persecution with them. The Latin American church has won credibility with those who desire to liberate the poor.

Others believe this retrenchment is good, or at least, necessary, since the church renewal unleashed by the Vatican Council has had some harmful consequences. As for the Medellín Conference, those who feel this way either ignore it, crudely attack it, or subject it to a slow death. (The teachings of Medellín were already being modified toward more traditional roles for the church by the time of the Third General Conference of Latin American Bishops at Puebla, Mexico, in 1979, although with only limited success.) They are suspicious of the model of the prophetic church — if not of its ideas, at least the way the ideas are applied. Thus they advise scaling back on the new model. But why this mistrust and fear?

Of course we cannot ignore the real limitations and faults of this prophetic church model, its exaggerations and one-sidedness, inevitable in such a widespread phenomenon. Nevertheless these problems can be controlled and remedied, and, anyway, they do not cancel out all the positive features of the prophetic church. To justify retrenchment on the basis of the prophetic church's limitations and faults appears to be more of an excuse than a true reason.

What then are the real causes for the retrenchment? In the first place the new model exacts high *costs*, above all, the divisions it produces within the church. No less important is the insecurity in which religious leaders have to live — because of their new place among the poor, because of their new relationships with the ruling classes (previously considered as the "natural" colleagues of the church), and because of the great creativity surging up from the grassroots church.

Second, there are *attacks* on religious leaders by the people in power when they side with the poor. These attacks are direct: threats, defamation, arrests, expulsions, torture, assassinations. They are also indirect: support and financing is turned aside from the church and put into otherworldly religious movements, as well as into more openly political neoconservative causes.[1] The attacks can be subtle, as when the church is praised as the defender of Western Christian civilization in order to keep its leaders from breaking their traditional alliance with those powers.

If we add to these costs and attacks the intrinsic demands of the new model of the prophetic church — for example, rethinking theology, living with the poor, abandoning social status — the present retrenchment of Latin American and Central American Catholicism is quite understandable.

The Prophetic Church as Threat

Those advocating retrenchment see the Roman Catholic Church as threatened from within, especially in Central America. The internal threats are seen as tendencies toward division, as doctrine that is less than orthodox (and thus dangerous to institutional stability and identity), and as unholy alliances with those old enemies of religion and the church: Marxism and the revolutionary movements.

To confront these threats the retrenchers insist on the importance of "church identity," understood as adherence to traditional orthodoxy as well as to the hierarchy. They consider Catholic Social Teaching[2] the only alternative to Marxism. In its present form, this teaching proposes "nonviolent reforms" instead of revolutionary models, which it sees as tainted by class "hatred" and inevitable conflict.

Allegiance to a strong hierarchy has become a priority for supporters of retrenchment. The hierarchy has also tried to regain control of grassroots church movements, which has led to some opposition between those movements and the institu-

---

[1]Many in the Central American prophetic church have felt pressured by campaigns supported by the Institute for Religion and Democracy. For a description of the role of the IRD see especially Ana María Ezcurra, *The Neoconservative Offensive: U.S. Churches and the Ideological Struggle for Latin America* (New York: New York CIRCUS Publications, 1983); Cayetano de Lella, "El papel del Instituto sobre Religión y Democracia en la ofensiva neoconservadora," in *Cristianismo y liberación en América Latina* (Mexico City: Ediciones Nuevomar, 1984), pp. 65–82.

[2]See note above, p. 54.

tional church. Supporters of retrenchment see the hierarchy as "the judge of society," with the church as the source of morality "above" all politics.

Of course, the Roman Catholic Church is not a static institution, and shifts in policy, practice, and personnel do take place at all levels. "Vatican watching" is a pastime with regional consequences for Roman Catholics and other Christians in Central America as well as elsewhere in the world.

The Religious Dimension of the Ideological Struggle. In a series of valuable studies, Ana María Ezcurra points out that the global counterinsurgency strategies of the U.S. in the 1980s regard the ideological aspect of "low intensity warfare" in Central America to be especially important.[3] In an attempt to respond to the growth of revolutionary movements that had both local and international support, the U.S. objective was to undermine this support and isolate the movements both nationally and internationally.

In these revolutionary movements, Christians and Marxists often worked together. Their sharing of ideas was important, but even more important was their cooperation on the practical level of helping the people organize. The Reagan administration as well as wide sectors of the churches saw this kind of coalition as a great threat. The question of Marxism has caused open confrontations within the churches, and the repercussions have reached beyond the churches.

Without doubt, the Nicaraguan case has become the best known example of the struggle over ideologies. Here Christians and Marxists joined in the Sandinista movement to overthrow the Somoza regime and rebuild their country on new political principles. Opposition to the Sandinista revolution has been vocal and powerful both within Nicaragua and in the United States.

Not only did the U.S. government mount military and polit-

---

[3]Ana María Ezcurra, *La ofensiva neoconservadora: La Iglesias de U.S.A. y la lucha ideológica hacia América Latina* (Madrid: IEPALA Editorial, 1982); *Ideological Aggression against the Sandinista Revolution: The Political Opposition Church in Nicaragua* (New York: New York CIRCUS Publications, 1984); *Doctrina social de la Iglesia: Un reformismo antisocialista* (Mexico City: Ediciones Nuevomar, 1985.)

ical opposition, but significant opposition has come from U.S.-based movements, corporations, and church groups. At the forefront of the *ideological* opposition to the Sandinistas within Nicaragua have been Roman Catholic groups — strongly supported by the newspaper *La Prensa*, the Reagan administration, CELAM,[4] Pope John Paul II, and some sectors of the Vatican, among others.

The Vatican Offensive against the Prophetic Church. Conservative trends in the church gathered momentum with the 1978 election of Karol Wojtyla to the Vatican as Pope John Paul II. In Central America, the new offensive by church conservatives became evident after the triumph of the Sandinistas in Nicaragua (1979) and the strengthening of liberation movements in El Salvador and Guatemala, but especially after Ronald Reagan became president of the United States in 1981.

The primary battles over ideas have been waged in the field of church doctrine. A leading conservative proponent since 1972 has been Cardinal Alfonso López Trujillo of CELAM, adviser to Pope John Paul II on Latin American affairs. The movement has been fed by many of the lines of thought developed by the neoconservatives and the New Right in the United States.

During his Central American visit in March 1983, Pope John Paul II called the prophetic church an internal adversary. This distorted picture of the prophetic church was meant to isolate and discredit it. According to the pope, the prophetic church has become a dangerous opponent because it is *within* the church, causing major conflicts and threatening orthodoxy and church unity.

It was not by chance that it was in Nicaragua that the pope spoke on this subject. The prophetic church in Nicaragua has meant a widespread participation of Christians in the revolution. Thus Christians have helped provide credibility for the Sandinistas and have made it difficult to depict the new revolutionary government as "totalitarian," Marxist, or "atheist," dedicated to the persecution of the church and religion. (To discredit the Nicaraguan government in just such ways has been the goal of the enormous campaign of disinformation and de-

---

[4]See note above, p. 49.

ception orchestrated by the media under the control of business interests and conservative church leaders.) The prophetic church in Nicaragua has also contributed to the development of less rigid positions, not only among the Sandinistas but also in other countries of the region, as well to exploration of new relationships between Marxism and Christianity, on both practical and theoretical levels.

A Common Policy for Central America. The political and ideological interests of the Vatican and those of the U.S. government in Central America are *not* identical. As we have said above, Catholic retrenchment perceived the prophetic church as an internal threat to the old model of Christendom. It saw the new grassroots movement in religion as divisive, unorthodox, and Marxist. On the other hand, the Reagan administration intervened in the region for fundamentally strategic security reasons. Yet Washington and the Vatican remained in accord about the identity of their common adversaries: liberation theology, the prophetic church, Marxism, the spirit of the Sandinista revolution, Central American revolutionary movements.

The visit of Pope John Paul II to Central America demonstrated those convergences, which had been apparent since early 1981. The reports of the Vatican diplomats in the region, of the most conservative Nicaraguan bishops, and of CELAM (in particular, of Cardinal López Trujillo) efficiently prepared the soil so that President Reagan, without the slightest blush, publicly asked for the church's support in promoting U.S. foreign policy objectives in Latin America in general and Central America in particular.

In an interview on June 7, 1982, Reagan spoke to the pope about mutual concerns in Latin America. He spoke of the U.S. desire to work closely with the church in this region to promote peace, social justice, and reform, and to prevent the spread of repression and atheist tyranny. On June 29 Pope John Paul II responded to a CELAM report issued in February and to President Reagan's request. In a letter to the Nicaraguan bishops, the pope condemned the "people's church" and Christians involved in the revolutionary process; he reaffirmed this condemnation, as we have seen, in his controversial visit to Central America the following year.

Rebuilding the Christendom Model

Beginning in 1981, a strong movement designed to rebuild the church-state alliance was apparent within Central American Catholicism; it stood in clear opposition to the movement that supported the new church model of Vatican Council II and the Medellín Conference.

At least three factors appear to have contributed to this attempt to restore the church of Christendom: (1) the effects of the brutal persecutions in the late 1970s and early 1980s, directed against progressive sectors of the church (primarily in Guatemala and El Salvador, but also in Honduras); (2) the increasingly powerful forces of retrenchment; and (3) the confusing effect that the process of "democratization," which was beginning to take hold in some countries of the region, had on many in the church.

In the first place, the persecution unleashed against progressive sectors of the church clearly reaped benefits for the Central American ruling classes. As a result of the persecution, the most dynamic structures of the Central American Roman Catholic Church were both morally and materially dismantled. Only the most conservative sectors and structures of the church were left intact. These later became the principal representatives of Catholicism in the region. In effect, the persecution generated traumatic fear that silenced many groups in the church that might otherwise have supported social reforms. That fear endures to this day.

Second, the groups that promote retrenchment, which largely control the Vatican Curia and CELAM, exercised great pressure over the weak and impressionable bishops of the region as well as over the superiors of the religious orders. They were pressured to avoid the "dangers" of the "people's church" and of liberation theology and to avoid conflicts with governments and with "friendly" groups in power, in order to preserve and even to reassert the institutional power of the church within these societies. For all practical purposes, retrenchment has been achieved: the more progressive church structures have been dismantled or at least controlled, and the bishops' conferences are for the most part more eager to please the Vatican

Curia or the authorities of CELAM than to respond to the needs of the people.

Third, during this period a policy of "democratization" enabled the Central American bishops to move forward in rebuilding the old Christendom model. The presence of civilians in the governments (especially if they were Christian Democrats, as was the case in El Salvador and Guatemala) made the repression seem less real to the bishops, or at least it made it seem less likely that the repression was a government policy or that the governments were responsible for it.

These factors — to which we should add the bishops' concern about the penetration and growth of new religious movements — created an atmosphere highly appropriate for rebuilding a neoconservative version of the old Christendom model of the church.

It is not yet possible to characterize this revised model of Christendom, for it still varies throughout the region. Furthermore, we must emphasize that retrenchment takes no single form. The sectors of the church that propose some "reforms" in society are different from the most conservative sectors, which want to return the church to its traditional status. Although both these sectors agree on such issues as the rejection of violence in grassroots struggles and non-confrontation with "friendly" governments (but support confrontation of "enemy" governments, as in Nicaragua), there are also differences.

So, for example, some who are open to reform support ideas like the "option for the poor."[5] Others reject such notions or reinterpret them in otherworldly terms, mostly because of their concern that many from the ruling classes who have felt abandoned by the church will desert it. Likewise, there are those who incorporate elements of the church of Christendom, for example, huge rallies, that others reject in favor of renewed approaches to ministry and worship. These latter groups rely on elements of the Christian base communities' experience, while seeking to purge them of any radicalism.

In sum, while in the 1970s there was a rapid progression in the region from conservative church structures toward a pro-

---

[5]See note above, p. 74.

phetic church model, beginning in 1981 a new opportunity arose for restoration of the old Christendom model.

The Bishops of Central America

Guatemala. The bishops conference of Guatemala is the most unified in the region. Although not all are equally close to the people, the Guatemalan bishops, especially in recent years, have presented a united front on defending human rights and indigenous people. This stance has led to confrontation with the military and suspicion by the most conservative sectors of the country. Nevertheless they have, for the most part, been able to stay on good terms with the government and the ruling classes.

The bishops have a generally negative attitude toward the revolutionary movement in Guatemala. They seem to take note only of the movement's errors and believe that it has no future. They believe that guerrilla warfare, far from solving the country's crisis, will again turn the indigenous people into "cannon fodder." But they are also skeptical about the social model proposed by the military and ruling classes. The bishops seem to seek a model of society based on "the common good of all Guatemalans," but are not clear about what this model would look like..

This "third-way" approach of the Guatemalan bishops explains their initial enthusiasm with the Christian Democratic government of Vinicio Cerezo. But they have become disillusioned with the government and so seem to have reached a dead-end.

The unity of these bishops is also a reaction to the growth of Protestant and evangelical groups in the country. Despite a rebirth of Catholic pastoral activity, however, this church has not been able to recover from the brutal repression it suffered in the early 1980s.

But a new spirit is now overcoming the bishops' paralysis. For example, they have played an active role as mediators between the government and the URNG[6] and have issued a valiant pastoral letter, "The Cry for the Land."

---

[6]See note above, p. 95.

El Salvador. Bishops recently appointed in El Salvador have supported retrenchment. Archbishop Arturo Rivera Damas of San Salvador, although he is no Oscar Romero,[7] has generally been able to maintain his progressive influence, and the more conservative bishops have not been able to overshadow his presence.

But the bishops as a group have no significant influence on the country. Although some bishops maintain a relatively independent stance, the official statements of the bishops have become ineffective — or easily manipulated by the government. Even Archbishop Rivera's mediating role has tended to justify inaction rather than critically and constructively influencing the conflicts from the perspective of the poor.

Indeed, the Salvadoran people expect more of their bishops. They want a more vigorous defense of those who have little or no voice, clearer condemnations of the abominations still being committed, and closer identification with their suffering. But such action has not been forthcoming from the bishops' conference.

Fortunately, the Salvadoran Roman Catholic Church as a whole walks more closely with the people who suffer, including those in combat. The church has been present in dialogues between guerrillas and the government and in prisoner exchanges. It has contributed to resettlement projects and helped distribute humanitarian aid. And it has maintained its Legal Aid office, which continues to document human rights violations.

Honduras. The Honduran bishops in recent years have taken a new, more critical stance. Not only did they call for the establishment of a National Commission for Reconciliation[8] and an end to violations of human rights and political corruption; the bishops have also been outspoken against the government and the military.

The diocese of Santa Rosa de Copán has been outstanding

---

[7]Archbishop Oscar Arnulfo Romero, archbishop of San Salvador and advocate of the poor, was assassinated on March 24, 1980. He is widely venerated as a saint throughout Latin America.

[8]Required in each country by the Arias peace agreement, to include government and opposition figures. The Honduran government delayed its establishment.

in its defense of refugees from El Salvador and of several persecuted priests, although only in the Santa Barbara area did it defend the repressed grassroots movement. The same courage was
seen in Yoro, in the archdiocese of Tegucigalpa, where a legal
aid office took up the cause of kidnapped peasants in Morazán
and El Progreso. Similar offices were created in other parishes,
and on the national level the bishops conference sponsored a
petition in defense of human rights.

The courageous actions of a number of bishops have won
respect from the military, who have no alternative but to deal
with the bishops' conference.

Nicaragua. In Nicaragua the conflict between the Roman
Catholic bishops and the Sandinista government has held center stage throughout the Sandinista years. The conflict has been
primarily political. Actions by the bishops intended to destabilize the political situation have been met with force by the
government.

The bishops' position has been based on the conviction that
the government is anti-Christian and can be overthrown. The
bishops demonstrated their rejection of the "atheistic enemy" in
their statements as well as in their call for the reversal of the
revolution.

The reactions of the revolutionary government appear to be
"tactical" errors, due to inexperience in dealing with religious
leaders of an institution as experienced as the Catholic Church.
The actions of the bishops, on the other hand, can be qualified
as "strategic" errors, for the Sandinista government has given
absolutely no indication that it is anti-Christian or that it can
be overthrown.

For now, tensions have eased somewhat, in part because the
Contras' military power began to decline in late 1985. Those
who had been convinced of the imminent downfall of the Sandinistas had to revise their assessment. Adept Vatican diplomacy
also began to change its strategy from open confrontation to
greater moderation, from opposition to dialogue.

There are also other reasons that explain this change. First,
the Nicaraguan bishops lost international credibility, mostly because Cardinal Miguel Obando y Bravo of Managua and Bishop
Pablo Antonio Vega, vice-president of the Nicaraguan Bishops

Conference, complied so openly with the Reagan administration's policy towards the Sandinistas.

Second, there was the contradiction between, on the one hand, the complicity or silence of the Nicaraguan bishops with regard to United States aggression against Nicaragua and, on the other hand, the U.S. bishops' repeated condemnations of the belligerent policies of its government as "illegal and immoral."

Third, the Roman Catholic Church needed to maintain its right to operate freely in Nicaragua, especially since the Protestant churches were not only growing in number but were also becoming closer to the Sandinista government. To maintain influence over its own members, the Roman Catholic Church needed to back off from direct confrontation with the government. Indeed, the majority of Catholics in Nicaragua had not complained about the restrictive measures that the revolutionary government had imposed on the church.

Costa Rica. Most of the bishops and clergy of Costa Rica come from a conservative or, at most, reformist mold. Initiatives by church groups or pastoral workers to build relationships with grassroots movements have been rare. And when they have occurred, the bishops have criticized them for turning pastoral work into politics, for distorting the gospel, or for introducing "alien" currents into Costa Rica.

The bishops have preferred to empower more "spiritual" specialized church groups rather than the Christian base communities. This allows them to avoid the "headaches" of a laity involved in social and political issues and to preserve the status of the clergy. The few experiments in grassroots ministry and church renewal that have been able to survive in recent years have done so within a kind of "hierarchical stockade," which has kept them from having any impact on a diocesan or national level.

The institutional church has been involved in social action only as a dispenser of social services for the welfare state or to fill the gaps in the reformist political programs of the National Party. The Costa Rican bishops have not shown any creativity in regard to the grave pastoral challenges: the world of the peasant, the complexity of urban life, the cultural values of the people. On the contrary, in face of the challenges posed by modern society, which grows less Catholic by the day, it has simply issued prohibitions. So it seems to be anchored to the past, satisfied with the institutional growth, social influence, and privileges it has already achieved.

The Complex Protestant Situation

Protestantism, both in its traditional and its evangelical forms, is now a highly complex reality in Central America. Many old classifications are no longer valid.

During the last two decades movements with worldwide outreach have appeared (ecumenical movements, charismatic networks, evangelical networks, neoconservative movements), which have crossed the traditional denominational lines.

The Protestant tradition of studying the Scripture and of lay involvement in the life of the church has been taken with new seriousness by some Central American denominations. The new movements in the Roman Catholic Church also have challenged Protestantism to redefine itself. Thus new ties with an "ecumenical Catholicism" developed, with ecumenical approaches to, for example, biblical interpretation and political involvement.

At the same time, the influence of the U.S. neoconservative spirit in many of these churches caused them finally to recognize the church's political role and abandon the fiction that churches can live "outside" politics.

In Central America today many members of the traditional Protestant churches suffer from an "inferiority complex" because of the growing numbers of Pentecostals. Moreover, the poor have migrated to the Pentecostal churches. Consequently, the traditional Protestant churches do not constitute a priority for the ruling classes. The Pentecostal churches have become more and more influential, and so there are more attempts by the ruling classes to manipulate these churches into providing credibility for the system.

The social and political situation has affected Central American Protestantism enormously. The revolutionary movements, the national security regimes, and militarization have polarized the churches. It is no longer possible for Protestants to be "in the middle."

Some churches have found a way to confront injustice in society by joining the campaign to defend human rights. Some have developed ministries to refugees and those uprooted by war, which have led to new links among the churches. Some Protestant Christians have formed active Christian base community groups, although they may call them by other names, or have joined their Catholic neighbors in forming such groups ecumenically.

The process of "democratization" has also figured in the mental outlooks of the churches; democratic language calls upon the Protestant conscience, since it is a part of the Protestant tradition. In addition, through their denominational and ecumenical links, the prophetic elements in the Central American Protestant churches have been vital sources of information and inspiration to Christians elsewhere. Mainline Protestant denominations in the U.S., for example, have spoken and acted strongly to move the U.S. government toward a more rational and just policy in Central America.

Central American Protestantism is a considerable social force that has fully entered into the political life of the region. In most cases, however, it has been on the conservative side. In any case it is clear that the present political situation in the region presents challenges to which the church authorities often do not know how to respond. On the grassroots level, nevertheless, very creative solutions are often found.[9]

The Churches Reorganize

As mentioned above, brutal persecution of the progressive sectors of the churches instilled traumatic fear in them, after which the most conservative sectors became the most prominent and vocal representatives of the churches. It is understandable that the progressive sectors considered the period of "democratization" that followed the difficult years of persecution as a respite for internal rebuilding of their ministries. With a deep suspicion that the armies were the real power behind the civilian governments, they preferred to take advantage of those spaces

---

[9]See Carmelo Alvárez and Carlos Tamez, *People of Hope: The Protestant Movement in Central America* (New York: Friendship Press, 1990).

available for ministry within the "opening" toward democracy.

At the same time, the rivalry over the Central American population, traditionally Roman Catholic, was accentuated by the presence of new religious movements (especially the "sects" and Protestant fundamentalists). According to various studies, these groups owe a great measure of their success to their ability to provide an oasis of escape, consolation, and distraction to a people afflicted by repression, war, and the daily problems of survival. For middle-class and business people, these groups offer a form of religion that protects them against having to question the way things are or becoming involved in social change. Belonging to these groups has become for many people — even some who were once involved in the grassroots movement — a way to survive by avoiding any suspicion of "subversion."

Roman Catholic lay movements have also grown. Besides those that have existed for many decades (for example, the Cursillo movement, the Christian Family Movement, the Legion of Mary), others have arisen during the 1970s and grown very quickly, for example, the Movement of Catholic Renewal. Such groups tend to imitate some of the techniques and at times even the theology of the sects and fundamentalist groups. Because the Bible has often been deemphasized in the Catholic Church, many priests and faithful accept these movements uncritically because they offer an easy answer to the need of many Catholics to hear the Word of God. Most of the bishops, although concerned with the "Protestant" character of some of these movements, particularly the charismatic movement, encourage or at least tolerate them because they believe that they can help stop the flow of Catholics toward the new religious groups. Furthermore, these groups generally practice an otherworldly spirituality and so act as a kind of "vaccine" against the prophetic church.

Although from the point of view of the grassroots movement these lay movements are usually considered part of the unjust system, not all can be judged in the same way. There are exceptions, and even some of the charismatic groups are open to justice issues.

Among such exceptions are the SINE program in Guatemala (Integral System of Evangelization), which in Costa Rica is called PESI (Process of Systematic and Integral Evangelization). More than a movement of lay spirituality, this program organizes evangelization and religious education on the parish level, and in some cases has taken a consciousness-raising approach. In Guatemala the Archdiocesan Commission for the Social Pastorate contributes to parish renewal through pastoral programs among the indigenous people or the Christian base communities.

Also important in Guatemala is the work of CIEDEG, the Conference of Evangelical Churches, which brings together the Brotherhood of Mayan Presbyterians, the National Methodist Church, the Full Gospel Church of God, the Evangelical Mennonite Church, the Nazarenes, and the Aguacatecan Evangelical Council for Total Development. The conference defines itself as an expression of church unity that includes service, theological training, and pastoral work. It combines the resources of several denominations and uses a prophetic pastoral approach that tries to help solve the country's problems.

In El Salvador, the Archdiocesan Social Secretariat is responsible for most of the social ministries of the Roman Catholic Church. The ecumenical organization called Diakonia coordinates social ministry for the Social Secretariat, the Lutheran Church, Immanuel Baptist Church, and the Episcopal Church, as well as two cooperative organizations.

The groups that form Diakonia began their work with agricultural, health, and educational projects for persons uprooted by fighting in El Salvador. Later they reached out to those affected by the earthquake of 1986 and, more recently to Salvadoran refugees returned from Honduras. Recently the Lutheran Church, increasingly important in El Salvador, established Lutheran Legal Aid, which has reinforced the human rights work of the diocese of San Salvador and the Oscar Romero Christian Legal Aid groups.

In Honduras, the Christian Development Commission supports development programs and grassroots education. The beneficiaries of these programs are Christian groups — both Catholic and Protestant. Important health education work is carried out by the Honduran Lutheran Church's EDUCSA (Education in Health).

In Nicaragua, the social pastorate of the archdiocese of Managua, generously funded by foreign sources, including USAID, is coordinated by the Archdiocesan Commission for Social Development, which maintains a close relationship with parties and forces opposing the Sandinistas.

Among the Protestants the development work and grassroots theological education carried out by CEPAD (Evangelical Committee for Aid and Development) are outstanding. This important committee, which brings together most of the Protestant churches of Nicaragua, generally supports the kind of educational and cooperative development programs advocated by the Sandinista government. It channels large amounts of foreign aid to the Nicaraguan people, though its programs principally benefit groups that belong to the member churches of the committee.

On the Caribbean coast the Moravian Church, which is the largest in the area, does important work in social action and education. The Inter-Church Center for Theological and Social Studies, with headquarters in Managua, also promotes development and education projects on the coast. Its goals are to improve communication among the churches, support efforts for peace, and contribute to the rebuilding of Nicaragua.

In Costa Rica a coalition of the government, pro-business political parties, and commercial interests carry on an unequal battle with the weak and besieged labor movement. This pro-business coalition has slowly spread to other Central American countries, especially Guatemala. It builds a worker-management structure that at every level is controlled by members of the business sectors. Its central tenet is that harmony between workers and management will increase production, promote peace among the work force, and better distribute the profits to both groups.

Some Roman Catholics, through the John XXIII Social School, vigorously support this pro-business coalition as a kind of "holy crusade" against the labor unions. The school thus gives religious credibility to the coalition. Furthermore, the workers belonging to the coalition receive a pro-business, anti-union interpretation of Catholic Social Teaching.[10] Since 1979 the school has concentrated its work in the Caribbean region of the country, particularly in the difficult banana industry. With the help of the large fruit companies it was able to influence significantly the labor scene in the banana industry. The coalition replaced the union and "direct agreements" replaced collective bargaining. In the eyes of union leaders and progressive politicians and church people, this development seriously damaged the credibility of the bishops, who have done very little to control this official agency of the church.

In early 1985 a new group of priests and laity was organized, convinced of the need for support from the Roman Catholic Church for the labor movement, whose survival was in jeopardy. The goal of this group, the Association of Labor Development Services, is to promote dialogue between the union leadership and the bishops and to train union leadership to deal with the challenge of the pro-business coalition.

Also in 1985 the Center for Evangelization and Society began to provide research services (for example, social analysis, parish census) to all the dioceses of the country to help them establish ministry programs.

In the same year the Federation of Costa Rican Evangelical Churches (FIEC) was organized as an alternative to conservative Protestantism. At present it includes twelve Christian communities, eight of them completely new groups in poor neighborhoods of San José.

The Prophetic Church and the Grassroots Movement

In *Guatemala*, grassroots organizations were weakened by the repression of the early 1980s. Nevertheless, they have begun to explore new possibilities. The first task, of course, is to survive repression and military control, now somewhat moderated under the Christian Democratic government of Vinicio Cerezo, but there are also efforts to rebuild the movement.

In these circumstances, the relationship of the prophetic church to the grassroots movement is, for all practical purposes, starting over. In the words of one prophetic church group:

---

[10]See note above, p. 54.

Often it was simply a question of silent accompaniment, simple gestures of support in the task of rebuilding communities in a kind of "ministry of hope" in the midst of despair. It was a relationship waiting for conditions of growth. Both parties realized that they were vehicles for forces that would later converge, in complementary tasks.[11]

A sign of promise for the Guatemalan prophetic church is the growing and creative participation of the indigenous population. With deep cultural roots and the painful yet hopeful memory of the widespread indigenous participation in the grassroots movement in the early 1980s, a good number of indigenous Christian communities are developing a truly independent church. Innovations in worship, ministry, and theology are beginning to appear, enriching the prophetic church.

In *El Salvador*, in areas under the control of the FMLN,[12] the ministry of pastoral workers has generally been respected. The FMLN has encouraged the link between the Christian communities and emerging grassroots organizations. Here the relationships between the prophetic church and the grassroots organizations have been direct and innovative. The challenge has been to find the balance between cooperation and independence.

In the territory under government military control, the prophetic church is also in a period of growth, although the circumstances are quite different. Since 1984, numerous Christian base communities have been established or reorganized. The members reflect together on the situation they live in, especially the internal war between the FMLN and the military, celebrate their faith, organize their ministries, and plan how they will work with grassroots organizations.

In *Nicaragua* the cooperation between the prophetic church and the grassroots movement goes back to the years of struggle against the Somoza regime. After Somoza was overthrown and the Sandinistas came to power on July 19, 1979, however, the relationship has been more difficult, and at times painful. Yet during this decade the prophetic church has matured. Living

---

[11]CAICA, *La Iglesia en Centroamérica: Elementos para una visión regional* (Mexico City: CEE, 1986), p. 11.

[12]See note above, p. 94

under a government that its members helped bring to power has meant that the prophetic church has had to look more closely at its own identity and mission. Living under a more sympathetic government actually made it more necessary for Christians to clarify their specific roles as Christians and their roles as citizens. I believe that this process of self-definition, of seeking its own role and learning from its successes and failures, has offered a special gift to the prophetic church throughout Latin America.

In the period immediately following the Sandinista victory, the prophetic church spent much of its energy dealing with the distrust, fears, and accusations of the Nicaraguan bishops. Moreover, the participation of Christians in the Sandinista revolution, although motivated by their faith commitment, did not appear to differ greatly from the participation of nonbelievers. There were attempts to clarify and deepen the Christian contribution to the revolution, but these attempts were limited.

Insofar as the bishops turned the focus of their opposition away from the "people's church" and toward the Sandinista government, the prophetic church could turn its energy toward the poor, whose suffering increased because of the U.S. economic embargo and the Reagan administration's policy of armed aggression. With this change of focus toward a "ministry of accompaniment,"[13] the prophetic church began to rediscover the value of religious practices such as fasting, prayer, vigils, and the stations of the cross. At the same time the prophetic church began a more balanced and fruitful relationship with the grassroots movement.

With the exception of Nicaragua (and to some degree El Salvador), at this time the relationship between the prophetic church and the grassroots movement is more a convergence of concerns than a formal organization. This convergence is based not only on common roots, but on the participation of the same persons in both the prophetic church and the grassroots movement. So, for example, many members of the Pro Tierra (For Land) movement in Guatemala, headed by Father Andrés Girón, are leaders and active members of the Christian communities.

Sometimes, of course, members of the prophetic church have

---

[13]See note above, p. 76

not only sympathized with local grassroots organizations, but have also supported them actively. But recent years have shown how necessary it is to recognize the autonomy of both the prophetic church and the grassroots movement. At the organizational level both groups have maintained some distance between the movements. Not only does such distance offer some protection against repression; it also honors the unique contribution each movement can make to a more just society.

When Christians of the prophetic church have blurred the distinction between themselves and the grassroots organizations, some groups in the church (and not just conservatives) have thought that religion and politics were "mixed up together." Then the church's message of liberating evangelization cannot be heard clearly.

It is very hard to decide what kind of relationship the prophetic church in Guatemala, El Salvador, and Honduras can have with the political and military resistance organizations in those countries. Clearly the repressive armed forces will not tolerate any relationship at all. So certain groups of the prophetic church refuse to make any public reference to the guerrillas. Yet, despite disinformation and lack of information, despite questions about the real power of the guerrilla forces and about their activities, their successes and failures, their political and military priorities, it seems that in general prophetic church groups have a favorable attitude toward the guerrilla organizations, or at least do not completely write them off.

The Marks of the Prophetic Church

Perhaps with less exuberance than in the 1970s and early 1980s, the prophetic church continues its difficult journey — tempered by the passage of time and well aware of its own sin and human limitations. Many see the prophetic church as the truth and the hope of the church of Jesus, as the path that must be taken. This new model of church has, without doubt, unleashed forces that cannot be turned back.

In the first place, we should not underestimate the church's *option for the poor,*[14] and all that it means. It is now the teaching

---

[14]See note above, p. 74

of the entire Latin American Roman Catholic Church, as well as the Catholic Church worldwide and many Protestant groups as well, notwithstanding repeated attempts on all sides to water it down by endless qualifications.

A second mark of the prophetic church is *persecution*. The stories of the martyrs are many and moving — not only the officially documented cases but also those kept alive in the oral traditions of the Christian base communities. They preserve the memory of the many Christians who in the last fifteen years have met death in their struggle for life. The Central American prophetic church is persecuted because it is considered subversive of a system of oppression and death and committed to the struggles of grassroots revolutionary movements. And in those movements the prophetic church finds a likeness to the Reign announced by Jesus. And so widows and orphans abound in Central America, among "the poorest of the poor." Their presence in large measure sets the priorities for the social ministry of the prophetic church.

Third, *Christian base communities* survive and grow despite great pressures, including persecution from outside the church and misunderstanding from within. They are repeatedly dismissed as the "people's church," the "anti-hierarchical" church, or the "Marxist" church. Yet these communities continue to show great creativity in ministry, theology, and worship. For example, they have developed a profound and striking appreciation for celebration:

> In the midst of war, suffering, and poverty, they do not abandon their guitars. They still come together to sing, in an atmosphere that, despite everything, is always festive and joyful. The number, quality, and beauty of the songs is impressive. These songs are being composed, in many instances anonymously, in the heart of a people that needs to express its hope and celebrate its faith.[15]

Fourth, active church organizations (for example, the various legal aid groups) *defend the lives* of the poorest and de-

---

[15]CAICA, *La Iglesia en Centroamérica: Elementos para una visión regional* (Mexico City: CEE, 1986), p. 17.

nounce human rights violations. Likewise many priests, ministers, sisters, and lay leaders carry out a dangerous ministry of accompaniment[16] in the mountains and other regions affected by the war. The refugees and displaced persons are also among the poorest, and their presence too is one of the marks of the Central American prophetic church. They are living testimony to the will of the people to control their own destinies, as well as to the repression of the powerful who will not tolerate it. They are signs to the churches of the faith of the exodus and of the journey in the desert in search of the promised land. At the same time they challenge traditional church structures. The Nicaraguan publication *Envío* describes their prophetic role:

> The Guatemalan refugees in Mexico, for example, have been able to put a positive value on their poverty; they have resisted offers to better economic conditions at the price of moving back to Guatemala and the subjugation that awaits them there.... The Salvadoran refugees, asked how they use their time in exile, responded: "We read the prophets and remember the passion of Jesus Christ" — which is to say that they keep alive their denunciation of a society of injustice, that their suffering is justified by their journey of faith in the crucified Jesus and vindicated in his resurrection.[17]

Moreover, there are heroic examples of Christians who are threatened and repressed, but who nevertheless remain with the poor.

Fifth, this prophetic church has not only passed through the test of persecution, but has also undergone a profound *maturation* as well. Without renouncing the struggle for justice, it has deepened its own spirituality. It understands more clearly what Christians can offer the movements for revolution: to defend the legitimate aims of the movements, to imbue them with a Christian spirit, to humanize them, and to help keep them from becoming rigidly dogmatic.

---

[16]See note above, p. 76.
[17]*Envío* (Nicaragua), 55–56 (1986), p. 71.

As theologian Hans Küng has well stated, groups in the church that favor retrenchment are ruled by fear that the church will be tainted by "ideologies," a fear that only stifles freedom and creativity.[18] The prophetic church, on the other hand, fears facing the living God on the last day, when God will ask what the church has done for the poor, oppressed, and crucified people of Central America. Indeed, these are the people the church faces every day.

The gospel demands that the prophetic church bear fruits of dignity, hope, communion, and joy. And so the prophetic church is necessary for the poor of Central America, since the church can give them hope and direction on their journey of liberation. And the church must do so — for God and for the poor themselves. Although the prophetic church is in the minority in Central America, it is the church that shows the greatest vitality, that best responds to the present challenges, and that represents promise for the future of the church in the region:

In this church we find the pearl of great price for which we must sell everything.... It contains the possibility of building a church faithful to the gospel of Jesus and the demands of the present moment. The weakness of the prophetic church in Central America is like that of the tiny seed: though it is small, it holds great promise. The social and political programs of the poor and the church programs that support them are barely a small seed. But without this seed the scene would be much bleaker than it is. For in this region rife with suffering and poverty, there is also a struggle going on to find new models of living together founded on dignity and equality. These models can provide a small light in a world that threatens life and the quality of life on many fronts. And in the same way, this new model of church that has already been born and is now developing in these countries can inspire the whole church.[19]

---

[18]Hans Küng, "El cardenal Ratzinger, el papa Wojtyla y el miedo a la libertad," in the supplement "Nuevo Amanecer Cultural," *El Nuevo Diario* (Nicaragua), 30, 9 (1985), pp. 1–3.

[19]CAICA, *La Iglesia en Centroamérica: Elementos para una visión regional* (Mexico City: CEE, 1986), pp. 21–22.

References

The author has relied especially on the following works:

CAICA. *La Iglesia en Centroamérica: Elementos para una visión regional.* Mexico City: CEE, 1986.

Dussel, Enrique. *Los últimos 50 años (1930–1985) en la historia de la Iglesia en América Latina.* Bogotá: Indo-American Press Service, 1986. In English see *The History of the Church in Latin America: Colonialism to Liberation.* Grand Rapids: Eerdmans, 1981.

Ezcurra, Ana María. *La ofensiva neoconservadora: Las Iglesias de U.S.A. y la lucha ideológica hacia América Latina.* Madrid: IEPALA Editorial, 1982. English translation: *The Neoconservative Offensive: U.S. Churches and the Ideological Struggle for Latin America.* New York: New York CIRCUS Publications, 1983.

Ezcurra, Ana María. *Agresión ideológica contra la revolución sandinista.* Mexico City: Ediciones Nuevomar, 1984. English translation: *Ideological Aggression against the Sandinista Revolution: The Political Opposition Church in Nicaragua.* New York: New York CIRCUS Publications, 1984.

Ezcurra, Ana María. *Doctrina social de la Iglesia: Un reformismo antisocialista.* Mexico City: Ediciones Nuevomar, 1985.

Gorostiaga, Xabier. "Horizonte geopolítico y teología de la liberación," in *Solidaridad* (Colombia), June 1988, pp. 26–37.

Gorostiaga, Xabier. "Perspectivas sociopolíticas y teológicas sobre la paz en Centroamérica," in *Amanecer* (Nicaragua), January–February 1989, pp. 31–37.

"Hacia dónde va la Iglesia," in *ECA* (El Salvador) 434 (December 1984), pp. 876–879.

Instituto Histórico Centroamericano. "El Nuevo Sujeto Histórico: Centro América 1979–85, El callejón sin salida de la política de EE. UU. en el Tercer Mundo," in *Envío* (Nicaragua), 55–56 (1986).

Jenkins, Jorge. *El desafío indígena en Nicaragua: el caso de los miskitos.* Mexico City: Edit. Katún, 1986.

Martín Baró, Ignacio. *Iglesia y revolución en El Salvador.* San Salvador: mimeo, 1985.

Mejía, Jorge Julio. "La coyuntura de la Iglesia Católica en América Latina," in *Pasos* (Costa Rica), September–October 1988.

Monteforte, Mario. *Centro América: subdesarrollo y dependencia.* Mexico City: Instituto de Investigaciones Sociales de la UNAM, 1972.

Pérez Brignoli, Héctor. *Breve historia de Centroamérica*. Madrid: Alianza Editorial, 1985.

Piedra, Arturo. "Evaluación crítica de la actual coyuntura evangélica centroamericana," in *Vida y Pensamiento* (Costa Rica), 1–2 (1984), pp. 3–20.

Richard, Pablo. *La Iglesia latino-americana entre el temor y la esperanza: Apuntes teológicos para la década de los 80*. San José, Costa Rica: DEI, 1980.

Richard, Pablo. *Morte das cristiandades e nascimento da Igreja*. São Paulo: Edicões Paulinas, 1982. English translation: *Death of Christendoms, Birth of the Church: Historical Analysis and Theological Interpretation of the Church in Latin America* (Maryknoll, N.Y.: Orbis Books, 1987).

Richard, Pablo. "La Iglesia que nace en América Central," in Cayetano de Lella, ed., *Cristianismo y liberación en América Central*. Mexico City: Ediciones Nuevomar, 1984.

Richard, Pablo, and Guillermo Meléndez, eds. *La Iglesia de los Pobres en América Central*. San José, Costa Rica: DEI, 1982.